THE NECTAR OF THIS BREATH

ALSO BY ALFRED K. LAMOTTE

Wounded Bud: Poems for Meditation
(2013, Saint Julian Press)

Savor Eternity One Moment at a Time
(2015, Saint Julian Press)

Shimmering Birthless, A Confluence of Verse and Image
(2015, co-author with artist/publisher Rashani Réa)

Fire of Darkness: What Burned Me Away Completely, I Became
(2019, co-author with artist/publisher Rashani Réa)

Nameless: Rashani Réa and Six Contemporary Poets
(2021, co-author with artist/publisher Rashani Réa)

SAINT JULIAN PRESS

POETRY

Praise for THE NECTAR OF THIS BREATH

"This is the work of a careful master and its breath will transform your life. As the author says, *we are here to die of love,* and it is this which holds us. The profoundly measured diction of these words is both weightless and transparent. LaMotte has achieved the work of a life-time in this book, and the precision of emotion and human intimacy is delivered with terrific sonority, poetic radiance, and integrity."

~Kevin McGrath, Harvard University, author of *Stri: Women In Epic Mahabharata* and poetry books: *Eros, Song of the Republic,* and *Windward.*

"This poetry is some of the finest, an invitation to the alchemical process of unveiling the gold you always were. With mastery and grace, LaMotte's verse activates an awakening process. His poems are passwords opening the heart, taking you to a wellspring of Divine essence that leaps from your own chest. You will not come out of Fred's book the same person."

~Chelan Harkin, author of *Susceptible to Light* and *Let Us Dance! The Stumble and Whirl with The Beloved*

"Images flow forth from him like mountain streams from the high peaks in Spring. He is the artist we love and long for, who reminds us that art itself proceeds from a divine source."

~Dorothy Walters PhD, poet, mystic, author of *The Goddess Speaks, The Kundalini Poems,* and *Marrow of Flame.*

"Alfred LaMotte's poetry is touching, beautiful, outrageously funny, utterly sublime. As Rumi and Hafez before him, he seems effortlessly to scoop Sacred Letters from his heart, and string them into beautiful Word Garlands for friends and beloveds. Through these poems we dive into the Bridal Chamber of the spiritual heart. Soaked in love and spontaneity, these magical spells are so powerful, even the dead will come alive and burst into tears, laughter, and ecstatic dance!"

~Shiva Somadev, author of *Journey into the Heart of Reality* and founder of Kumbhaka Prana Yoga.

"Opening this book is like opening the door of a temple, to imbibe holy sacraments and anoint oneself with the miraculous. These words break open the mundane shell of our existence, revealing the immaculate spirit within. Nothing escapes these portals of revelation. Every wound becomes a doorway into vibrant truth, every shadow a gateway into the light. With words that drip with endless joy and devotion, he peels back the veil of the ordinary, revealing the sacred Heart at the center of existence. These poems not only enchant and illuminate, they also teach the reader how to see."

~Maya Luna, author of *Omega: Feral Secrets of the Deep Feminine* and creator of The Deep Feminine Mystery School.

"Here are poems with lines I whisper every night into the ears of my 4 and 7-year-old sons, to endow their psyches with wild truth and magic. Here are poems I text to ten friends at once, moved by an uncontrollable inspiration, only to receive back waves of awe and thanks for the blessing of Fred's spells. And here are poems who are living companions, made of such rascally, heartbreaking love I'm called again and again to climb out of my old skin, and in that glistening sensitivity, to shine."

~ Brooke McNamara, poet, Zen Dharma Holder, author of Feed Your Vow and Bury The Seed.

Alfred LaMotte's poems are beautiful inviting bridges to contemplative silence and meditation. Paradoxically, they wake us up and comfort us at the same time. As the pandemic unfolded, Fred's poems helped our Heart Centered Meditation group calm anxiety and strengthen connection to one another, inspiring our reverence for life. They offer a felt experience of the world we want to co-create, grounded in awe of the sacred.

~Elizabeth A. Walz, Executive Director, Genesis Spiritual Life and Conference Center

THE NECTAR OF THIS BREATH

Poems

by

Alfred K. LaMotte

SAINT JULIAN PRESS
HOUSTON

Published by
SAINT JULIAN PRESS, Inc.
2053 Cortlandt, Suite 200
Houston, Texas 77008

www.saintjulianpress.com

COPYRIGHT © 2022
TWO THOUSAND AND TWENTY-TWO
©Alfred K. LaMotte

ISBN-13: 978-1-955194-02-0
Library of Congress Control Number: 2021949958

Cover Art Credit: Marney Ward
www.marneyward.com

INTRODUCTION: A BREATH BOOK

Sweep up the dust of a thousand ruined civilizations in this breath. Gather the ashes of your ancestors in this breath. Whisk the DNA from all the microbes that ever swarmed the gut or swam the blood of rodent, honeybee, or leprous medieval peasant in this breath. Reap the protein from each virus, harvest molecules of leopard scat and wolverine, the very color code of parrots in this breath. Garner the rune of an alien chromosome, fossilized in meteorite, or learn the secret gene-Om of a black hole humming at the core of a distant sun, from this breath. Distill the tears of your enemies, the wild scent of your first love from this breath, the healing elixir in rain-forest herbs, dew from the eyes of your unborn children, the bittersweet atoms that Jesus breathed. Now hold and cherish this breath, sweeping up the stories, the grievances, the blame and forgiveness. Transmute it all into sparkling awareness.

This is a breath book. Let it lie by your bed or meditation seat, poems that explore the liminal space between verse and guided meditation. A poem should be a useful tool, like a hoe. The handle need not be fancy, but well-worn, easy to grasp. *Use* these poems to awaken the angel in each inhalation, and remember that we all share one divine breath, who dances through billions of bodies. Savor one poem at a sitting. Let it lead you to the *So'ham* meditation taught by ancient yogis: breathing in *So*, the Divine, breathing out *Aham*, I am. Dip into the well of this moment and draw up the gift of silence, the gift of tears, the gift of laughter.

Laughter? Yes, spirituality is a "debate between reverence and irreverence," to quote one poem. Hearty irreverence liberates the Spirit. Along with contemplative poems here are robust incantations to be shouted or chanted aloud, my homage to Whitman and the Beats, who were feral bards of breathing too.

A Goddess haunts these poems. We don't breathe, we are breathed. She who breathes us is the Great Mother. She is called Shakti in India, Shekinah among Jewish mystics, Sophia Wisdom and Holy Spirit in the Church. We regard breath as an autonomic biological function, which of course it is, until we ferment it with consciousness. Then it is a sacrament.

We are born to breathe Spirit in a body. Spirit and Breath are analogous words in both Biblical Hebrew and Greek. The book of Proverbs personifies divine Wisdom as a woman who was with God in the beginning: "When He set the heavens in place, I was there" (8:27). She is the divine breath of creation.

"By the word of the Lord were the heavens made, and all their hosts by the breath of his mouth" (Psalm 33:6). The two aspects of God's creativity are Word and Breath. Christian Gnostics like Valentinus saw here the masculine and feminine: Christ the Word, Sophia-Spirit the Breath. We find the same male-female synergy in the Yoga tradition of India: Lord Shiva and his consort, Kundalini Shakti. Shiva is the silent witnessing aspect of God, Shakti the active pulse who sets the heavens in motion and breathes through our flesh. A classic yogic text, Vijnana Bhairava, declares, "The supreme Goddess, whose nature is to create, constantly expresses herself as exhalation and inhalation. By resting awareness in the space of the heart, between the descending and ascending breaths, one experiences Bhairava, the source of creation."

In the West, God's Word and God's Breath find human expression in Jesus and the Magdalene. The Gnostic Gospel of Phillip describes the sacrament of the "Bridal Chamber," where the masculine and feminine powers with the human soul are wed. "In Christ's Breath, we experience a new embrace; we are no longer in duality, but in unity… All are clothed in light when they enter the mystery of the sacred embrace."

Friend, these poems are about this very wedding in your heart. She who sent the galaxies whirling in their circle-dance has come to dwell in your body as this inhalation. Nothing is more ordinary, yet more miraculous. Uniting all religions, the sacrament of breath is humanity's first worship. Why not flood every cell with an ocean of love, and immerse each strand of DNA in healing waves of the Spirit? The original prayer is simply to rest the mind in the heart, and follow this breath Om.

DEDICATION

To my teachers, Maharishi Mahesh Yogi, Sri Sri Ravi Shankar, and the lineage of the Shankaracharya tradition; to the Mother Goddess in all her forms, Shakti, Shekinah, Sophia Wisdom; and above all to my beautiful ever-nurturing wife Anna, thank you.

CONTENTS

SECRET . . . 1
ANCESTRY . . . 2
HUMMING . . . 3
HYMN TO IMPERFECTION . . . 4
STRANGERS AND PILGRIMS . . . 5
MUSTARD SEED . . . 6
INVENTORY OF ESSENTIAL DISTRACTIONS . . . 7
THREE MIRACLES . . . 8
ELECTION . . . 9
SHEKINAH . . . 10
ONE LAW . . . 11
PRAISE SONG . . . 12
NO CHAKRAS . . . 13
CARNIVAL OF DRUNKEN POETS . . . 14
FOUR A.M. . . . 16
SAY LESS . . . 17
BRING THOUSANDS . . . 18
DOING BUSINESS ON THE SABBATH . . . 19
SADHANA . . . 20
TO THE GARDEN . . . 22
OLD TIRE . . . 23
LITTLE CREATURES . . . 24
STAR SECRET . . . 25
MAGI . . . 26
TEA WITH A LADY OF ZEN . . . 27
LOGIC . . . 28
A CHILDHOOD PRACTICE . . . 29
CAN YOU BOW? . . . 30
NATIVITY . . . 31
ATTENSHIN DEFSIT . . . 32
THE SIMPLEST MEDITATION . . . 34
JUICE . . . 35

HOW IT BEGINS... 36
SWAMP SUTRA... 37
WIND HARP... 38
CATASTROPHE... 39
WILD FLOWER YOGA... 40
DWINDLING DAYLIGHT... 42
SOME SAY YOU ARE NOT THIS BODY... 43
LISTENING... 44
THE PRACTICE OF WINTER... 45
KOAN FOR A SUNDAY MORNING... 46
WHAT SHALL YOU WEAR?... 47
WEDDING... 48
RETROGRADE... 49
KISS YOUR DEMONS... 50
ALL I CAN DO... 51
POEM IN THE SHAPE OF A GRAIL... 52
AWAKE... 53
YOU MUST DANCE NAKED... 54
TIRED OF GODS... 55
SACRED LAND... 56
NON CREDO... 57
ODE TO YOUR HANDS... 58
MIDSUMMER'S EVE AND MORNING... 60
PARTNER... 61
WORLD WITHOUT US... 62
CHANDRA NADI... 63
WHAT HAPPENED TO WELLS... 64
JASMINE... 65
ODE TO YOUR HEARTBEAT... 66
SALMONBERRIES... 68
IF YOU PRAY... 69
COLLAPSE... 70
PLEDGE... 71
GOSPEL... 72

DO ANY KINDNESS . . . 73
TRASH: A SABBATH MEDITATION . . . 74
WHAT HAFEZ WANTS . . . 76
A DARK WORLD . . . 77
FUCK UP . . . 78
MEN . . . 80
EULOGY FOR A FINCH . . . 81
MERELY METAPHYSICAL . . . 82
OCTOBER WALK . . . 83
ESOTERIC MATHEMATICS OF THE SRI YANTRA . . . 84
GRAND ALIGNMENT . . . 85
MISSION . . . 86
A SIMPLE RELIGION . . . 88
SHRAPNEL . . . 89
THANKSGIVING FOR MY SKIN . . . 90
FOOL . . . 92
LIES . . . 93
THE HEALING . . . 94
IMPORTANT TO SAY . . . 95
TO REMIND YOU . . . 96
OUTLAW . . . 97
BARE BRANCH . . . 98
A MORATORIUM ON NAMES . . . 99
PIE . . . 100
VOCATION . . . 101
AMAZEMENT OF GARDENERS . . . 102
RETURN . . . 103
WOUNDED FLUTE . . . 104
BRUISE . . . 105
SONNET IN AUTUMN AIR . . . 106
THANK YOU . . . 107
HOW TO FALL ASLEEP . . . 108

THE NECTAR OF THIS BREATH

SECRET

It's almost midnight.
I'll tell you a secret.
You are the candle,
God is the moth.
And just as your flesh
has a soul,
so your inhalation
is a sheath
containing a sword
of sweet fire.
Plunge this blade
into your heart.
You are here to die
of love.

ANCESTRY

My DNA results came back.
Just as I suspected, my great great grandfather
was a monarch butterfly.
Much of who I am is still wriggling under a stone.
I am part larva, but part hummingbird too.
There is dinosaur tar in my bone marrow.
My golden hair sprang out of a meadow in Palestine.
Genghis Khan is my fourth cousin,
but I didn't get his dimples.
My loins are loaded with banyan seeds from Sri Lanka,
but I descended from Ravanna, not Ram.
My uncle is a mastodon.
There are traces of white people in my saliva.
3.7 billion years ago I swirled in hydrogen dust,
dreaming of a planet overgrown with lingams and yonis.
More recently, say 60,000 B.C.
I walked on hairy paws across a land bridge
joining Sweden to Botswana.
I am the bastard of the sun and moon.
I can no longer hide my heritage of
raindrops and cougar scat.
My mud was molded with your grandmother's tears.
I was the brother from another tribe
who marched you to the sea and sold you.
I was the merchant from Savannah
and the cargo of blackness.
I was the chain.
Admit it, you have wings, vast and crystal,
like mine, like mine.
You have sweat, dark and salty,
like mine, like mine.
You have secrets silently singing in your blood,
like mine, like mine.
Don't pretend that earth is not one family.
Don't pretend we never hung from the same branch.
Don't pretend we do not ripen on each other's breath.
Don't pretend we didn't come here to forgive.

HUMMING

Before the invention
of thoughts
we sang ourselves
to sleep.
The day melted back
into humming,
the humming into silence,
silence into a breath
of the Beloved.
Of course the stars
were not yet born,
and the moon was still
inside you.
Lay your head
on my shoulder now.
Listen with all
your heart,
and I will teach you nothing.

HYMN TO IMPERFECTION

Stars confess the unendurable fire
of their longing for You.
Your body is their journey's end.
No need to be a pilgrim anymore.
No need to ascend.
Just be a touch of fallen sunset
on the face of the blind Bengali widow
selling Kumkum at the trolly stop
beneath the Durga statue.
Or get lost in the murmur of desultory frogs
entwined in fetid delight among
the mud-sprung water lilies.
After ten thousand lifetimes you'll grasp
what a robin knows at sunrise:
how to sing without trying.
Ask a thistle seed, "Do you have
a plan for the wind?"
Love is not a method or a path.
Just rest in the ancient lineage
of the present moment
and keep whispering, "Grace, grace."
There are thousands of reasons
to doubt, but only one breath,
many hungers, but a single wanting.
We starve for forty nights,
then get drunk on a buttercup.
We become dusty mirrors just
to polish one another with forgiveness.
Fall softly through the blessed void,
an awkward braid of honeyed wine
splashing into a dark chalice.
Even your jagged edges are made
from infinitesimal love-sparks.
Why did the Maker break your wings?
To teach these feet to stumble.
You can't thank Her enough, can you?
Now throw away your measuring cup,
the world is a sea of gratitude.
You dive in with your whole body,
then come up gasping with a soul.

STRANGERS AND PILGRIMS

"And they confessed that they were strangers and pilgrims on the earth." ~Hebrews 12

You have pilgrim eyes,
the second sight of a stranger.
And the lens through which you see
is the broken place
in your body,
which is the broken place
in your soul,
which is the world
you see.
And when you meet
another wanderer,
you break open
even wider.
You remember how she
is the world
in the shape of a wound.
You see her through
your shattered lens,
which brings her into focus,
which is how you
heal the world;
not by long suffering
some collective dream
of global despair,
but by intimate encounters
on the labyrinth way,
one pilgrim at a time -
and by breathing
through your broken place
into hers.

MUSTARD SEED

The space beyond the sun,
over the swirling rim
of the Milky Way,
is the hollow in the mustard seed
that was planted in the furrow
of your missing rib.
You overflow the chalice,
therefor breathe the night.
You are so ancient,
your glow is still approaching
like a promise, like a pilgrim God,
and you are still receiving
your name.
How do I know this?
I don't, I taste it.
Someone touched
the soft spot on my crown
and poured the nectar
of emptiness
into my bones.
I won't say who,
but her scent is pungent
with star-pollen.
Her exhalation shimmers
with the radiance of the dark.
If I were one of those
soul merchants
Who sell keys to the door
that is always open,
I would bottle her perfume
and call it
"Bewilderment."

INVENTORY OF ESSENTIAL DISTRACTIONS

Titmouse at a thistle feeder.
Wing-beat of geese
navigating by the moon.
Exultation of a turquoise moth
who will die before sunrise.
A baby's ancient gaze
from a supermarket shopping cart.
Honor the essential distractions
that make you whole.

Gifted by the mist at dawn,
shards of sunbeam trembling
in the open fingers of a fern.
Elegant cracks in a hand-made tea bowl.
Choir upon choir of empyrean petals
in a fallen camellia.
Are we not redeemed by the sure
sweet vision of particulars?
What else is faith?

Glistening spider's web
in the withering hyssop.
The motionless explosion of a rose.
Every flame-tipped thing conspiring
in a ceaseless whisper of revelation,
"Yes, you are here."
Waves dissolving on sand.
Silence between raindrops.
This breath.

THREE MIRACLES

Begin the day
with three miracles.
Savor your first breath.
Cherish your heartbeat.
Let diamond silence crystalize
between your eyebrows.
You will break open
like a ripe seed, and the earth
will flower out of you.
Raindrops, wind, and pebbles
will do the rest.
Your feet will be frolicking leaves.
No path is needed.
When you hear a sparrow,
your heart will fall in love again,
I promise.
Very well then, don't choose
a single paramour, take billions.
Like countless reflections resting
on one clear mirror, petals
in an amber calyx,
the faces of strangers will appear
as lovers because they repose
in the eye that is looking.
Something like a braid of sunbeams
will twine up your backbone,
spilling over, golden
as the stuff in Mary's womb.
Nothing can be ordinary
if you start your morning with miracles.
Now drink up the rest of this day
and squander the Kingdom!

ELECTION

I voted.
I voted for the rainbow.
I voted for the cry of a loon.
I voted for my grandfather's bones
that feed beetles now.
I voted for a singing brook that sparkles
under a North Dakota bean field.
I voted for salty air through which the whimbrel flies
South along the shores of two continents.
I voted for melting snow that returns to the wellspring
of darkness, where the sky is born from the earth.
I voted for daemonic mushrooms in the loam,
and the old democracy of worms.
I voted for the wordless treaty that cannot be broken
by white men or brown, because it is made of star semen,
thistle sap, hieroglyphs of the weevil in prairie oak.
I voted to keep the edges of the vineyard
ragged and ungleaned for the hungry stranger.
I voted for the local, the small, the brim
that does not spill over, the abolition of waste,
the luxury of enough.
I voted for a motherland where politics dissolves
into folk music, story-telling, fermented cabbage,
totem-carved hoes handed down from mother to son
in the fire-side silence of heroic listening.
I voted for the commonwealth of the ancient forest,
a larva for every beak, a wing-tinted flower
for every moth's disguise, a well-fed mammal's corpse
for every colony of maggots.
I voted for open borders between death and birth.
I voted on the ballot of a fallen leaf of sycamore
that will not be erased, for it becomes the dust and rain,
and then a tree again.
I voted for more fallow time to cultivate wild flowers,
more recess in schools to cultivate play,
more leisure, tax free, more space between days.
I voted to increase the profit of evening silence
and the price of a thrush song.
I voted for ten million stars in your next inhalation.

SHEKINAH

Don't imagine that breathing
is something you do
just to stay alive.
Breath has a secret purpose.
As you fall asleep tonight,
honor this inhalation
like a royal guest.
Make a spacious tent of your flesh,
for she who ripens the moon
and harvests clustered galaxies
has come to dwell in the desert of your body.
She will make you an oasis for the stars.
She'll kiss your baby pate and pour
Laneakía down your spine.
Let intoxication lead you
to her moonlit door.
The key is silence, step through.
Follow her rainbow into the void,
where wings of amazement
will carry you from death to death.
A scent of myrrh and balm of Gilead
in the garden of the unborn
will guide you home, enlarged
by a memory of stillness.
If you want to awaken the angel
in every breath,
forget your name in hers.
Not knowing
is the space of compassion.
Let her pull you down into the seed.
Empty your stem, fathom your sap.
If you won't become hollow,
how can you be filled with music?

ONE LAW

When a mother lives in the street
and sleeps on the sidewalk
in front of your brownstone,
you need many laws
to keep you safe.
They all say the same thing,
"Stay away."
But when you invite her inside,
you recognize, indeed,
she is your mother,
the one who brings this breath.
She sits down by the hearth
where your grief is burning
and you give her something warm to sip
from the old iron cauldron
you've carefully kept from
beating too hard, like your heart.
You notice, indeed,
there are many cracks in it now.
And you remember, it was she
who gave you this bowl,
just as her mother gave it to her.
Then you discover
that only one law is required,
the one that says to every stranger,
"Welcome home."

PRAISE SONG

Praise the local, the native, the small.
Look what springs out of last year's garbage.
Who needs a committee?
Who needs Republicans or Democrats?
Look what springs out of
coffee grinds and beetle dung.
Who needs capital letters after their name?
Praise the local, the native, the small.
Who needs Goldman Sachs or the Federal Reserve?
Look what gets polished by worms.
Look what springs out of
broccoli crowns and yam skins.
Who needs borders? Who needs an enemy?
You have a community garden
full of neighbors in old hats.
Praise the local, the native, the small.
Why waste one atom of energy
being "against"
when you could be "for"?
The revolution is to breathe.
The radical act is presence.
Look what springs out of your heart.

NO CHAKRAS

When I laugh I have no chakras.
The sun is my heart.
When I cry the moon comes down
to caress my forehead,
but finds no lotus to kiss open.
Breathing the Beloved's scent
clears my natal chart
of every planet and sign.
The astrologer is bewildered.
All he sees in me is an empty page
full of light.
Don't give me any more of your
esoteric books.
Grace has made me too stupid
to understand.

CARNIVAL OF DRUNKEN POETS

Ran into Kerouac at the Carnival of Drunken Poets,
where those just dead meet those about to be reborn.
Jack and I have wandered through the zodiac, prodigal suns
under the 13th sign, the sign of inebriation in the house of Lilith,
with Coyote rising, the Moon single and pregnant again.
We meet here every 26 thousand years.

The heavenly huckster sees us coming and shouts: "Step right up!
Watch gladiator-poets beat each other silly with roses.
One will die of wounds that gush communion wine!"
The crowd is ferocious, hungry for metaphors.
I bow to Jack, Jack bows to me.
We make the fatal mistake of opening our mouths.

"Gorilla lilies at my Resurrection!" he wails.
I refute him, "We forbid the silly physicists of tantra
to taste our semi-sweet chakras,"
to which he replies, "I spin galaxies of cotton candy
from the dark matter of God's breath."
I demand, "What overflows the hexagon of your hollow grail?"
He answers, "Honey from the horny void!"
I shout, "Supernova crème brulée!"
And Jack replies, "Why should the midnight hummingbird
not sip rainbows from my wounded eye?"
I insist, "Nanno-galaxy in the groin of an electric frog!"
Jack says, "A medicine woman must dance in your thalamus."

It's no use, I'm weeping now, as Jack, the master sommelier,
whispers, "Dip the brackish water from the womb, extract
the secret chi, burn the afterbirth as inexhaustible green fuel."
I can only reply, "Drop a song of worms into the beak
of my feathery daughter as she stumbles into the sky."
Jack murmurs, "When I set the loaf of my body on fire,
God will blow out the flame, I will become snow."

Then I shout: "Broken motors of the pharmacopoeia
dripping petroleum in the rainforest of your neurons."
But he answers, "Subatomic Obama!"
I moan, "May insect helicopters infest the Amazonian
Chacruna leaves in your President's ayahuasca."

Now the mind-police prepare their post-modernist bonfires.
I attempt a more rational inquiry: "If Mary Magdalene consumes
the body of the Lord, then exhales the vaporized brandy
of his ascended flesh, what shape is frost on memory's window?"
He says, "Dissolve in the April of the heart and taste your tears,
then confess that love and pain have one flavor."
But already the crowd has lit the pyre, shouting by torchlight,
"Burn the Bodhisattva who exuberates our bellybuttons!"

Epilogue: The Death Of Kerouac...
They bind the lamb-white French Canadian football star,
cat lover, bhikkhu of cheap wine; his bone-smoke dims the sky.
O sound of neon thrush eggs crackling in the 12th House!
O clangor of rose-window dragonfly wings shattering spacetime!
O keening of genetically-modified caterpillars with no eyes!
Kerouac's marrow a cloudy holocaust of rainbows
unfolding the eleventh dimension of my adoration,
the pavonine horizon of his beatnik smile, staining the dome
of eternity with fractals from the tip of Shelley's tongue,
with Whitman's teardrops, Attic dust from Keats's urn.
O terrible cathedral of similes, those crystal arches of death,
curve-yearning to kiss the one Platonic asymptote of beauty.
Gone, Gone beyond, Bodhi Svaha, O vanished Jack.
O mad pretender of Zen, embodied shaman spell, now only
an unpunctuated rain of ash descending among cedars
on a Cascade trail to Desolation Peak, over the Salish Sea...

Friend, here's the truth about your radiance:
If you want to turn the Spirit green, you'll have to thrust
your sunbeams through the belly of an earthworm.

FOUR A.M.

If you knew
how inconceivably near
the moon is to
this pearl of silence
in your forehead,
threaded by the finespun
sparkling dew
of pure attention,
if you knew
how many elixirs of love
you imbibed
with your last inhalation,
how many potions
of healing you'll pour out
through your next
astounded sigh of praise,
you would awaken
before dawn
to spend the darkest hour
in radiant stillness, simply
caressing the earth
and bathing the stars
with this breath.

SAY LESS

True listeners open the ear in the heart.
They love the gossip of raindrops,
the breaking news of Spring peepers.

Say less than you mean.
Grace is the gift of subtraction.
The trembling crystal of a chickadee
proclaims the whole Godspell.

Tell as little as a willow by a pond
where the heron glides away
on the first breath of twilight.

And if you must speak, leave
a rippled stillness between words,
the kind of mirror where
that long-beaked huntress might pause

on one leg all a golden afternoon.
Be more like the moon between clouds,
until your silences say everything.

BRING THOUSANDS

I know the world hurts.
But there is a very safe place
right here where
your breath arises,
your heartbeat is born,
and the moon drinks
all the light she needs
from the bright stream
of your silence.
Rest here.
Don't be afraid.
And don't come alone.
Bring thousands with you.

DOING BUSINESS ON THE SABBATH

This Sunday morning, before dawn,
I invested in the silence of the unopened rose.
I sold everything and purchased emptiness.
Even the amber atoms of my flesh
I threw into the deal, they became
pure light, and lost their market value.
I could only dance.
With a single glance I sold the stars
and galaxies for nothing.
I put stock in hollowness, and became rich.
Oh I admit, it was insider trading.
Jesus spoke of such ruthless transactions,
the commerce of the void.
"Love will make you poor," he said,
but everyone thought he was talking
about politics.
This is what he meant, friend:
never bargain with the Beloved.
Only the destitute get paid.
Declare bankruptcy
and be done with it.
Find the treasury of stillness
and sell everything.
This is how you do business on the Sabbath.
I lost my shirt, my body, the earth and sky.
Then the sun rose like a bubble
playing on an infant's lips,
weightless mountains floating
in delicious snow, sea and shore
a trembling mirage in the wealth
of a teardrop.
I traded my armor and shield of iron
for inestimable nakedness.
I belong to someone else now.
Everything's been sold
to the master of amazement.

SADHANA

Gaté Gaté Pará Gaté Parasám Gaté Bodhi Svahá: Gone, Gone, Gone Beyond, Gone Beyond Beyond, Hail the Go-er! ~Buddhist Mantra

Spent thousands for enlightenment at the Ashram
of Tantric Wine Tasting, advanced Tai Chi
at a seaside resort in Bali, $1200 room
with a complimentary green smoothie.
The bronze yogini on the cushion next to mine
has a blissful smile. Did she get a better mantra?
I'll never perfect the Peacock Asana.
I need a Wounded Raven Pose.
Breathing in, say "in," breathing out, say "out."
But why not say "My Polish grandmother
rides her electric scooter through golden atoms
of intergalactic chicken broth?"
Here's the koan I could never solve: "Can you replace
the concept of that lady's rump with No Mind?"
So I took my complaints to the Guru, who laughed and said,
"When did you ever see *me* doing any of that crap?"
Then he threw his arm over my shoulder and led me
to the Taproom of Laughter, where everyone
gets instantly drunk by practicing absolutely nothing.
His head inclined on my chest, he murmured,
"Don't call me Master any more, call me Friend."
There I met Jesus and Rumi, Hildegard and Mirabai,
Walt Whitman and Ferlinghetti, all passing one enormous cup,
in which were many grapes, but a single sweetness.
I couldn't tell the hobos from the saints.
Each night there's a lively debate between reverence
and irreverence, stillness and dancing,
which always ends uproarious guffaws.
The bartender asks no tip but a wine-drenched kiss.
At the entrance, millions of gods stand in line, all claiming
to know someone inside with a human body.
I'm sure they'll get in, because they hear music and love to dance.
We leave our knowing in the lobby with our shoes.
None of us has the slightest idea who's giving the party.

*

I must be getting lazy, lost my longing
for exotic spiritual destinations.
Just want to wander in the woods beyond
my dilapidated fence, listening to raindrops on ferns.
No dakinis painted inside my skull, no Tibetan calligraphy
on the limestone cavern of my emptiness,
no more vanilla dharma talks by some guy named Levine
who calls himself Ananda now.
I must be getting old, just want to sing about
the vastness of what I don't know,
and open the third eye on the bottom of my sole,
pressing dark loam with a barefoot kiss.
From where I stand on the slow-turning earth,
I can see that "here" is already "there,"
this Dharma Wheel rolls nowhere, the hub is stillness.
I'll honor the moss-bearded cedars, very great gurus,
who offer their priceless teaching for free: a mist-green quietness.
The roots of their lineage truffle down to the seed of creation
entangled in the fungi of the void, close to the fountain
of bewilderment that gushes from the center of each now.
Listen friend, a teacher fills you, a Guru empties you.
A teacher transmits knowledge, a Guru awakens the knower.
A teacher bestows information, a Guru bestows wonder.
The mind thirsts for certainty, the heart yearns for breaking.
If the yearning is intense enough, the Guru could be a cricket.

*

If you still need rules to follow, follow these.
Bow to your grandfather's enemy, kiss the ground.
Vow to be healed by the very next stranger.
Walk softly on earth, sipping from the barrel of foolishness.
Pulverize diamonds with your whirling....
It's midnight, I hear the incantation of Her who meant
to ululate the color green, but accidentally sang the stars.
Soundless owl wings slice the glory of darkness, bright knives
of un-knowing, moonlight seeps from my wound.
I am thrice awakened: in me, in you, in the gut of an earthworm.
Parasám Gaté, beyond the beyond, right where I am.
Coyote howl will be my song.

TO THE GARDEN

Whose breath rolled the stone away?
Who entered the tomb to discover
brightness in the vacuum?
It was you.
Now the dead poet, Jesus,
wanders through this vineyard of bruises
plucking remnants of the harvest
from the trellis in your ribs.
He is famished, unhoused.
He wants his bone hammer back,
to be a carpenter again.
Isn't it time to let him know
what he has become:
the nameless warmth in your marrow,
generous as morning?
You are the bud, he is the season.
The invisible nectar of his lips
has empowered you.
His faintest exhalation makes the Eye
of Sauron Galaxy condense
like mist on the windowpane
of your abyss.
You are his whisper now,
your quietest prayer a whirler
of constellations.
You are the sound that the Magdalene hears
in the garden at dawn
when she is too amazed to answer.
You call her with the music
of the clustered hive, the honey-makers
murmuring, "Ameen, Ameen."
Now your task is only to surrender,
pervade, un-imagine distances.
You are the way to the garden.
You are the opening of the gate
that was never closed.

OLD TIRE

*Many know the use of the useful, but few
know the use of the useless.* ~Chuang Tzu

A family of possums
living in an old tire,
waves of morning glories
drowning an abandoned Chevy.
Who plants flowers in a junkyard?
No one, friend.
They plant themselves.
I would rather love the smallest good
than resist the greatest evil.
A robin, too ardent for outrage,
weaves her nest from threads
of dangling moss, dead twigs.
The moth does not protest
the evening of the world.
A honeysuckle's silent trumpet
conquers the night
with a drop of dew.
What are you resisting?
Here's the revolution:
Be open to the kiss of rain,
the sun's caress.
Release the fragrance of vulnerability
and bees will return.
Make your home in an empty circle.
See in the dark.

LITTLE CREATURES

So your animal spirit guide
is a panther? A bison? A bear?
Mighty powers, my friend!
How often, on a Winter morning,
do they come to your window?
I prefer the wisdom of little creatures.
My totem is a hummingbird.
Her wings instruct me to discover
the highest vibration in stillness.
Her delicate bill invites me
to sip and get tipsy
on the amrit in my chest.
Once I believed in my thoughts.
I could not escape from the kingdom of fear.
Then this tiny turquoise thing of air
shattered the ampule of my wound fragrance.
Somewhere in these petals of fire
there is nectar for the one
who is not afraid of drowning.
She taught me to perish with every breath,
and live in eternity.

STAR SECRET

Stars have a secret.
They are always tumbling
into orbits of glory.
They do not attempt to fly.
Darkness is their wing.

If you don't believe me,
you are still trying
not to fall.

Plunge more deeply
into the womb of night
and you will draw very near
to the radiance of your Birth.

Ah, so this after all is a poem
about the Nativity?
Now bend and listen.

You are not here
to save the world.
You are here to discover
that you Are the world.

You are compassion.
You are healing.
In you the mountains
are lighter than the sky.

Don't try to understand this.
Just fall in love with yourself
in every pair of eyes.

And however you may worship,
take a blessed breath
of the newborn light
that is never even one
moment old.

MAGI

Wise One, drop the reins
and let the camel guide you.
Follow the rising falling animal
in your chest.
To be wise, after all, is to be led
across the wordless desert
of prayer
to the birthplace in the valley
between breaths
where the unspeakable
holds silence in a tiny hand,
the furry dust of the barnyard
dances in a moonbeam,
and a lady gazes into the hay,
with a look not so much
of adoration as bemusement,
as if nothing could ever
surprise her again,
She whose void was moist
with stars, and prior to conception
gave birth to radiant darkness,
with joy and sorrow mingled
in the milk of her dugs.
Impossible rays ascend
from the feeding trough,
filled with a tumult of hope.
What gentle chaos can it be?
How did you find this place?
You dropped the reins.
You followed the rising falling
animal of your heart.
To be wise, after all, is to be led.

TEA WITH A LADY OF ZEN

"Sometimes I'm too lazy
to meditate," she said.
I said, "Maybe diving deep
into laziness
is your meditation."
She sipped her green tea,
not silently, but with a slurp
of gratitude.
"As for me," I said,
"I'm a poetry bum.
I can't bring myself
to do anything useful."
"Maybe diving deep
into uselessness
is your meditation," she said.
Her tea was brewed
so subtle and clear
I could hardly taste it,
and I didn't know how
to make that wabi slurp
of satori suchness.
My failure erupted as laughter,
then a tear of thanksgiving.
Suddenly, without trying,
we savored a breathless quiet
which somehow polished the moon,
immersing the planet in tenderness,
dissolving the sorrows
of ten thousand creatures,
and guiding the stars home
to their perfect repose.
We danced in the emptiness
of each other's eyes.

LOGIC

I believe in logic.
A tree frog lives in the folds
of the old umbrella.
Therefor it will not rain today.
And because we are in love,
2 x 0 = 1.

With a little cream, I am scattering
fresh blueberries on my oatmeal.
Thus the hurricane changes its course,
and peace comes to the city.

Precisely at the feathered gong
in a red winged blackbird's throat,
a dragonfly lands on a cattail
quivering on the edge of the bog.

This can only mean that
the world is good, it is very good,
and the wetland must abide
for a thousand years to come.

And because you are troubled
by almost everything, my dear,
despite the ceaseless golden pulse
of grace that breathes you
out of the dark, you shall be
perfectly human.

A CHILDHOOD PRACTICE

Sometimes you want everything
to start over.
You remember how the gate
to her garden swung
on the hinge of your heartbeat.
So'ham…
You remember how to take,
no, receive, one breath.

This is the stream of gratitude
that bathed us all in the beginning.
It is what silence does to the warbler's breast
at the kiss of dawn.

No vow, no sacrifice required.
Just keep pouring the ghee of attention
into the flame of your belly,
thrilling distant stars.
You remember now,
this jolt of coming home
to the body,
and how it seems
to be the whole sky.

Sometimes you want everything
to start over, and you take,
no, receive, one breath.
So'ham…
There now, it's done.
And the world is new.

CAN YOU BOW?

Can you bow like a broken necklace, scattering
your brightest tears? To bow is the first asana.
All yoga postures simply remove the stiffness
so that you can bend in freedom.
Don't just bow to a master, bow to a grain
of pollen like a bee. Genuflect like a thirsty
panther drinking from a pond at sunset.
Bow to Spring like mountain snow that melts
into brook laughter. To the sound of a tree frog
in a jasmine vine at midnight, bow down.
To the plums of September thumping the ground,
showing you the way to fall, the way to split open
and offer your juice, bow down.
Bow to the silence of the doe who after all
is eating your roses. To your own breath, bow.
Fill the hollows of your body with the sky.
Bow so completely that you shatter your crown
and sow the earth with stars. Bowing is a sacred art.
God bows to the Goddess in the bridal chamber
of your heart, the binaural pulse of awareness aware
of its own radiance, its Self almost an Other,
a rhythm in the One. Let your knees grow weak
with the power of this melting. Let your forehead
strike sparks of grace in wet soil, evanescent galaxies
bending toward you before you were born, each
atom of the cosmos saturated with thanksgiving.
But remember, gratitude is not a practice.
Your bow was already here, pervading the night,
conceiving your flesh to humble its curved space
with gravity. Therefor bow to your mother and
your father. Bow to your child, to your teacher,
to your ancestor and his most terrible enemy.
Bow to a ladybug, a cricket, blue emptiness.
But please remember, this is not your bow.
Bowing is a gift of grace, a first cause.
Your bow is God, bowing to you.

NATIVITY

Mid-Winter morning. A befuddled kitten
marvels at the fallen whiteness, and the pawprints
that seem to follow her everywhere.
A junco, perched on the snowy head of Francis,
patiently waits his turn at the feeder, sunrise
in scattered angel wings flecked on a frozen pond.
Cherubim thirst for a body like yours, made of
vanished galaxies, yet casting a shadow.
They envy the way you found the nest inside the egg,
a mother's womb encircling her savior.
They worship an infant too. Any child will do.
Which is the whole point, isn't it? The triumph
of birth despite the poverty of Winter light?
It happens in a Palestinian haybarn, or a tenement
in the South Bronx, the name of the baby, Miguel
or Jesus, JaDawn or Billy Bob. If there were no Christmas,
you would have to invent one just to remind yourself
that you were divine on your birthday too, delivered
in a sack of salt water and blood. Ah, but your breathing
was thistledown, angel pollen in your hair, God-particles
in your pee-pee, bones all marrowed with gold,
potent mantras, "Ma! Dada! Kali! Ga!" erupting from
your reptilian brain, dissolving the gap between heaven
and earth in sacred burps and farts, starry spirals
blossoming from chinks between the vertebrae you
twisted and arched in pudgy asanas: the chuckling Serpent,
the dainty Plow, furrowing your pink baby fat, the hollow
Unicorn pouring moon-milk through your fontanelle...
And is this why you visit five-star ashrams?
To mimic the mudras of the newborn, to loll on
a yoga mat and recollect crib gestures, the secret sadhana
of infancy: how to suck stars through your belly button?
This fine Mid-Winter morning, why not bow to any baby's
marshmallow toes? Receive the Holy Name: a giggle
from her lips. Heavenly enough, how the triumph
of last night's snow reposes in glistening impermanence.
Wherever this melting leads you, friend, go there.
Each breath is Mary, and just to be awake is Christ.

ATTENSHIN DEFSIT

For all those who graduate and all those who don't, written after refusing to flunk my most interesting and incomparable student, though he earned an F. The poem attempts to capture the internal narrative of the student with severe learning disabilities. Forgive if I offend. Forgive your children too.

Got a D+ in English, in French almost a C.
They say my diagnosis is Hyper ADD.
In Math I got D-, and all the rest were D's.
My learning style is different, like Socrates'.

Like Moses. Like Beep Beep the Road Runner.
I love the desert and the mountain top.
I got a B+ in Snowboard and a straight A in Hope.
I don't smoke dope.
I'm not a geek.
My learning style is just unique.
Hey nonny nonny and a hey nonny nee,
Balloon Man whistling far and wee.
Verily verily I say unto thee,
Bishmillahi Rock Roll a Marine.

In the name of Yahoo begotten not made very doggerel
from very dog the square of hippopotamus is the sum
of Yin Yang plastered over the golden dome inside my skull
as I lie on my back staring up at mosaic Hebraic adreno-cortical
graffiti squirted from my hypothalamus scrawling dopamine
equations that generate all possible functions of X all faces
of god staring back at me from my own third eye third yoni
third planet from the sun of yes know seeing Me see Her
singing hey nonny nonny and a hip hop Beep Beep Shema
Ye Wassail Adonai its all one with no punctuation!
D-... Rewrite... Beep Beep...

I have seen the best minds of my generation destroyed by SAT's
the sacred imagination starving hysterical naked abused by PHD's
in corporate mind control administered by the Department
of Multiple Choice I have seen tectonic plates in my cerebellum
quaking flaming fissures on April 15 when the letter from
Stanford did not arrive at Mother's house or Father's house...

I've seen souls deranged by the logic of the immaculate
totalitarian paragraph the bloodshot sophomore ghosts
of November riding Ritalin home estranged in fear
to face the all-night alcoholic AP Faulkner novel ticking
with clocks of sound and fury signifying nothing...

I have seen the ghosts of Puritan fathers hovering over
Neoplatonic linoleum desk tops with whips of religion
whispering names of New England colleges I have seen
America's bankers brokers lawyers Ken dolls secretly yearning
to lie on nap-mats after milk and cookies sucking their thumbs
and dreaming of the Eleusinian kindergarten...

I have seen the heavens and the bald earth crowning
from a womb of shadows in the hands of Midwife Sophia
the dream of dark matter anti-matter and it-doesn't-matter
woken by the natal cries of God's most sacred Tetragrammaton
A-D-H-D bursting thousand-petaled skies in each neutrino...

Now I lay me down to fall and wake to taste-touch-smell-see all
my multitude of starry selves in the holographic quantum bijou
of this Christic moment when my mind can finally breathe
the bright and broken symmetry of Zero gushing particles
of night O fountain and fecundity of emptiness whose one
mad myriad Yes! gives birth to all the ruckus of my heart
my love's black beams of praise pulsating gems of ruby
from the diastolic stillness of the pomegranate Void.

THE SIMPLEST MEDITATION

The simplest meditation
happens when you hug
every cell of your body.
They all dissolve in one
gentle breath.
There is no other.
Consuming the thinker
in her own sacred
flesh-flame is called
the opening of the heart.
Now there is nothing left to do
but frolic with stars
and waltz with the moon
through an ever-widening
luminous swirl of compassion,
which is the space where
your darkness gives birth to the sun.
Was there a path? Ah yes,
it led you in all directions at once,
like a small blue flower
unfolding, touched
by the dewdrop of bewilderment.
Adoration is the fragrance
of your Being.
Now sing and play in the highest
world, which is this one,
where you learn to say Yes.
Yes to aloneness, to snow,
to the scarlet berry of pain.
Where you learn to behold
your face in the gaze of a stranger.
Go outdoors and play in the rain.
Play more intensely, as children do,
making it your work.
Risk amazement.
Love until there is
no other.

JUICE

When you opened your eyes this morning,
you broke every law that made yesterday real.
Why insist on being who you were
before you took this breath?

Can you withdraw your kiss, or send the ocean
streaming back to mountain snow?
Do bees bring their vintage to lavender
murmuring, here's the pollen I borrowed?

Nipples of columbine ooze nectar
for the hummingbird, then wither with contentment.
So let your chest be an inn for wandering rhythm.
Welcome the stranger, the angel of your next inhalation.

You must die of sweetness, like a pilgrim
who never comes home. This is the Law.
Don't ask the vineyard's forgiveness.
Grapes won't understand why you crushed them.

Once the madness starts, be choiceless.
Bold naked feet have danced on your heart too,
pulverizing all your stories into a fermented sigh.
This traumatic grail is empty now, and bittersweet.

Mingle with the galaxy. Discard your husk.
The bubbling stuff you have become will never
be nectar again. Can you withdraw your kiss?
Juice is for children. Jesus loves wine.

HOW IT BEGINS

Don't tell me about the end of the world.
Tell me about the beginning.
Befriend entropy.
Assume this exhalation is your last
and you are on the slope of a final heartbeat.

Be a wing that glides on gravity, rising
only by surrender, never quite knowing
how this melody is made from listened silences.

A thousand skies are raveled in a raindrop,
a thousand lives of wisdom in a tear,
last Summer's light on a brittle twig
wrapped in a milky cocoon, a blue egg
waiting in its mother-swirl of sticks,
she too the shaper of galaxies.

Relax into uncertainty, into the wound
of not knowing, into the sound
of what happened before creation
in the brilliant beginning-less core
of this moment.

Come taste and see
the diamond-pointed bindhu
between the mirrors,
between the world and its beholder,
here, where what flows out
meets what flows in,
a tiny wild flower of grace
that glows only an inch or two
in front of your chest.

Don't tell me how it ends,
tell me how it begins.
How this breath is given
because you surrendered that one.

SWAMP SUTRA

Your little green spirit guide
is calling, "Thank you, farewell!"

He is making the holy pilgrimage
from his dahlia pot on your back porch
to the golden skunk cabbage
in the wetland

where he will join the amphibian chorus
to become a quaver of pure
terraqueus delight
in the emerald Sangha,
rehearsing the Swamp Sutra
for their April concert.

O Dharma seeker,
do not form a concept
of True Emptiness,
but truly empty your mind
of concepts.
Then simply listen, listen,
and you may hear what they are singing:

"Love is Wiser than a Raindrop's Kiss
and Sadder than Sunrise in a Mist of Roses
when You Are Nothing
but a Frog."

WIND HARP

In an empty haybarn
an abandoned
wind harp hangs,
welcoming
the sojourning breath
of a summer afternoon.
So it is with a body
at rest.
The wandering breeze
selects her pine,
a moonbeam chooses
its trillium to caress
among the ferns,
and some ancestral yearning
settles on your mother's spine.
How supple she was,
undulating to receive you.
When you agreed
to her darkness,
what were you seeking?
The density of starlight?
The secret touch of snow?
Now it's time to remember,
time to let your soul
become pure listening
again, and your flesh
the song of the wind harp.

CATASTROPHE

We're like dead bees
in each other's goblet
of raindrops.
Three billion years ago
your atoms and mine
fell hopelessly in love.
Why stop falling now?
Abandon your vows
and follow wonder.
Flow towards what you adore.
Assume that the catastrophe
has already happened,
this dumbfounding explosion
of what we have become,
and the end was the beginning,
when every lover caught fire,
vanished in the burning,
in the place where breaths kiss,
and there is neither coming in
nor going out.
No I, no Thou remain,
but One more luminous
and crystalline, more
faceted and whole,
One who cares more carelessly
for both.
We're just the ashes floating back.
What do a seed, an egg,
a lyre, a plum bud, lips half-parted
have in common?
They do not resist.

WILD FLOWER YOGA

No one teaches yoga to a flower.
Learn bending from her stem,
the supple power of green
no hurricane can crush.
Breathe from the seed.

Without a sequence or routine,
your body is a river of postures
flowing toward the ocean of repose.
The zephyr of this breath
rests like a feather on your belly.

After so many years of practice, can you
give up formal poses and just move
to the rhythm of begonias in late October?

Rooted as a weathered oak,
can you sway with the seasons
of in-pouring and out-pouring,
ligaments softening in the void,
a starry wheel rolling out of your chest,
the axis of the galaxy poised
between your paps?

Can you dance with the Beloved
even when you are alone,
your backbone Kali's wand,
your pelvis her boat, laden
with its cargo of moonbeams?
Can you let a serpent pierce your heart?

The mind does not survive her thunderbolt of silence.
All that remains is the flesh.
Your eyes tell beads of gratitude,
pearled on a wordless tendril of exhalations,
and the fierce name of your Mother
protects you from the shadows of false light.

Dear one, there are intricate
miracles of attention
woven into the quivering sinews
of your heart, each nerve threaded
to a certain ache of sweetness
in the meadows and the woods.
You wander in the wilderness at midnight.
You trust in the candle of breathing,
stepping softly into the next lit pool of faith.

Keep it soft, friend, like the mystery
of gristle in a baby's crown.
That is the door you leave by,
made whole by lost drops.
Be a connoisseur of tears.

From your sacrum to your fontanelle,
a hollow nerve of liquid lightning hums.
Follow it Om to your toes.
It's your own dance now.

No more instructions.
Micro-movements invent themselves.
Majestic spirals of molten stillness
swelling from caverns of marrow.
The sutras are your bones.
No one teaches yoga to a flower.
Breathe from the seed.

DWINDLING DAYLIGHT

Dwindling daylight, dark by five.
Bore down to root-glow,
petals returning to the seed,
prayers withering into meditation.
If you kiss your shadow at this time of year,
something ignites. The Feral Lady,
single mother of the dawn hour,
visits your secret chamber, the space
between the self and its knower,
where new worlds ring in bejeweled blackness.
What you call falling, she calls the dance.
What you call the wrong note,
she calls stunning harmony.
You say "mistake," she says "creation."
By Springtime, her musk
is on the heather, blood on the moss.
"I return," she says, "when you return.
If you choose me, I have already chosen you."
She visits all the bistros on this road,
The Crown, The Heart, The Coccyx.
Once at the Inn of the Unspeakable
I saw her face beneath the shimmering veil
of absence, sequined with stillborn moons.
I felt her dagger of silence slitting the throat
of my name. All my drowned questions
floated like corpses on her gaze,
and I became a river of stillness, sweeping
old stories into the abyss of now.
She lured me like a selkie, down
into the oceanic bulb of her golden poppy,
this cauldron of transfiguration,
where She changed the dark heart of my flame
into sap, into the terrible sweetness
that does not need to breathe.
Now I know that wherever we are
is the Tavern of Awakening.
If you meet her there, mention me.
Tell her I remember.
See if she smiles.

SOME SAY YOU ARE NOT THIS BODY

Some say you are not this body.
I say you are made of such distant suns
their light is only now arriving as your flesh.
I say the fiery dark abyss devouring time
is the well of your next inhalation.
And if you do not rendezvous with God
in a crow-footed wrinkle or a liver spot,
or glory in the petals on your stem of thorns
in this aching fallow-fallen meadow, how
will you taste the bloom and fade of lips
on the heavenly Christ Rose?
Why count your years when the number
is always One at birth and death?
Just sink into a molecule, where every
proton in your ancient hologram of blood
is threaded to its native star.
Gown your naked soul in love-silk.
Let each electron bathe in the glory
of its origin, each quark collide with
the darkest particle of its other self.
Be pollen floating in the beam of what sees,
be the death-spiral of microbes in loam,
black vacuum at the axis of all that whirls.
I say you are this body, descended yet risen
from loss, from yearning so chthonic
no god could fall here, never having
tippled the sky in a chalice of ashes,
or sipped wisdom from one atom of a corpse.
As for auspicious birth-signs, there are three:
your chance meeting with a blind vagrant sperm,
a star-stuffed blastosphere encrypted
with secret Gnosis by fallen angels,
and the carelessness of your mother
concerning the moon…
Now use the faintest feather brush
of breath on bone to dust the mind away,
and be the silence that has all along
been listening to your prayers.

LISTENING

All day long your mind hears
the twit and chatter of the world.
If you pay attention to the mind,
you will become what it hears.

All day long your heart listens
to listening itself.
If you pay attention to the heart,
you become the sky,
and deep inside, the crescent moon,
the evening star.

Once you called it hopelessness,
now, ineffable beauty.
Don't you know that your silence
is the womb of fearless singing,
and your world is only made
of the distance you must travel
to find yourself?

Now bend to hear
the one breath in all creatures.
Feel the place in the fern forest
where a wounded doe
gives birth,
and bones move under fur
like an ancient loom.

THE PRACTICE OF WINTER

Those who visit this world
report that it is a planet of chaff,
rind, stretch marks, scar tissue.
Everyone here must break open,
wear a gash on the belly to reveal
the bewildering sweetness of their fruit.
If you can't find passion
in a land of disappointments,
at least be ardent about this breath
as if it were the gasp of one just born.
Then softly attend your sigh
as if it were your father's last.
The practice of Winter requires no effort.
Simply do not fear the hollow places.
Be thankful for what's left in the gourd,
for the gift of withering, your
opening palm, your persimmon cheeks.
Find another word for emptiness.
Look for the pods, the husks,
bright crinkled faces in the Void.
If you can find that starless seed,
where it's always too long ago
for you to have been born,
you will become what ripens
on a jagged branch, still hard and bitter.
Assume that you lie dormant in an old
growth forest, where December
is having you as her dream.
Now what is your name, your form?
Are you the soundless owl
or the crimson pulp of entrails
glistening in snow?
Whatever is delicious,
whatever is astounding,
whatever is ruthlessly alive,
blossoms and dies this moment.

KOAN FOR A SUNDAY MORNING

"Layam vraja: dissolve now!" ~*Ashtavakra*

Here is the beginning
and end of prayer.
Don't count beads,
dissolve them.
Don't count breaths,
dissolve them.

Don't count the hours or years,
dissolve your journey now.
Don't count your faults
or the sins of the world.
Dissolve them in the beauty
I Am.

Now here is a koan
for a Sunday morning.
Is there any more healing balm
that you could possibly pour
upon this hurting world
than simply to repose
in your body,
allowing all creatures
to be merely themselves?

A flower can feel it,
blossoming in stillness.
A cloud knows it,
moving through silence.
Why then do you have
so much trouble
just dissolving into what
You Are?

WHAT SHALL YOU WEAR?

What shall you wear to the wedding?
Be the moon with no mantilla,
the sky without a cloud,
the blues that stain a lover's thoughts.

Savor the gossamer illusion
of the wound around your heart.
Let the silence of this breath disclose
the sweetness of irremediable loss
by refusing to tell a story about it.

Why not rest in devastation,
and repose like a burnt lamb
on the naked alter of your breastbone?
Let others make the haj.
Your task is being hollow.
To the cup it feels
like something that pours,
to the wine, like stillness.

Did no one ever teach you how
to die with each exhalation?
Or how to see your mother's hand
in the golden veins of an alder leaf?

Fear was for another life,
this one is for wonder.
What shall you wear to the wedding?
Just this luminous veil of joy
with no one inside.

WEDDING

There's a feast between your nipples.
I think it's a wedding.
Powerful vows are spoken here,
where the sun gives the moon away.
Anyone who says "I do"
gets crushed,
danced on like a grape,
and changed into what
they were thirsting for.
It doesn't matter if you lost
your invitation.
Just show up.
The doorkeeper will let you in.
Tell him, "I'm homeless and parched.
I only came for the free food,
the last best jug of wine."
Now the doorkeeper is God,
who is very very lazy.
All he does all day is let people in
like a mirror.
Just give him a steady gaze
until you see the ancient smile
of your own heart,
playful as the turquoise curve
of eternity.
In your next inhalation,
feel the rose gold garment
of his grace upon you.
He'll speak your name so softly,
the way Jesus said "Mary"
in the garden.
Then you'll remember, sure enough,
it's your wedding!

RETROGRADE

Stop crying, "What should I do?
Mercury is in retrograde!"
What you should do is
dance like the sky.
All horoscopes tell one story:
the universe is your reflection.
You are a swirl of sun, moon,
and planets with your own
feral rhythm, hardly a waltz.
No map of the sky can
teach your body how to dance.
Those chimeric spheres and
jejune baubles are just wind chimes
in the illusion of distance,
all moved by one breath, yours.
Don't get burned by little sparks
falling through the night.
Be the conflagration.
Seven billion birth charts
singing the same chorus:
"You are made of fire."
Leo, Capricorn, Taurus, Aries,
patient beasts of blackness
roaming through the meadows
of your flesh, munching karma.
They are not above.
"Above" is a buried bulb
in the dark between heartbeats.
Galaxies bunched on
the arbor of your spine
ripen their golden orbs into amrita.
O seeker, drink the vintage
of pure awareness.
Ferment your stars into That!

KISS YOUR DEMONS

This is a good morning to kiss your demons.
Give them the kiss that Jesus gave Mary at the tomb.
Don't drive them away or they must return.
Why fear them? They are only your dark angels.
Lust is not a demon but a dark angel of moon sap.
Anger is not a demon but a dark angel of healing fire
flickering in your pons. Grief is a dark angel
bearing seven oceans of love in one jar.
The angel of Depression keeps vigil with Wisdom,
binding her Tartarean bones in nutritious mycelia.
Kiss one, and free the other.
Addiction is a dark angel bringing gifts
under a broken wing, using the other to help you fly,
for one of yours is broken too.
Bow to your dark angels, embody them.
Breathe them until they become sighs.
Possess them, or they possess you.
Exhale boldly and they vanish
in the blue sky of awakening, a swirl
of hummingbirds, a sound of tree frogs
discussing everything under the sun.
But beware of Enlightened Ones with no dark angels,
who lead you into the shadow that hides from itself.
Kiss them too, and depart.
Let their names and teeth marks, hieroglyphs
scrawled in the veins of your liver, neurons
twisted into Sumerian runes, spells thrumming
your medulla, rippling the gristle in your omphalos,
untangle their tongues and sing themselves back to silence.
May the wickless flame of your lips consume
all your dark angels, and lick your spine clean
with the kiss of soul upon soul.
Now swim down the river of amazement that flows
from the cavern of your hidden grief, over scars of stone.
This is the starless wine of ancient midnights
fermenting the sun of tomorrow.
This is the wine Christ saves for the end of the feast.
How do I know?
I am kissed.

ALL I CAN DO

All I can do for you is take your hand
and softly lure you to the quietness
that surrounds your wound,
enfolding the remnant of this breath
in what is so hollow it glows.
No sorrow survives that emptiness.
It is like a mirror.
Look, I am holding it up for you.
Now slip into the Witness,
insouciant beauty who ravishes
the motionless night with whirling.
Be the raven native to your brain,
dancing at the golden core of your thalamus.
If you have no faith, use mine,
this shattered beaker of bone,
trickling a pathway from sepulcher to sea.
Fling your heart into orbit around stillness.
Be the un-tethered gaze
that sees from every star, encircling
absence with wider absence.
Let loss be the illuminated door.
Hush now, the eloquent don't cry.
Catch a full moon
in your trembling web of patience.
Taste a scarlet berry in the void.
They father fire who fall in love with darkness.
What if your path does not lead
to the next moment, but deeper
into this one?
Be the Winter sun in a white seed
offering her shadow back
to what was never created.
Even That is who you are.

POEM IN THE SHAPE OF A GRAIL

Don't waste a single exhalation
complaining about the world.
Just choose beauty and sing.
The gift will not appear
until you are grateful.
Under the snow,
seeds listen.
The softer
your voice of praise,
the more they reach their
empty purple cups
of yearning up.
This is the art
of thirst.
Creation happens
in quietness.
You are a garden,
your breath is the Spring.

AWAKE

As you awaken, just before
the mind of yesterday falls
like a net of stones behind your eye,
be weightless.
Be Presence without a story.
How your soul looks in that mirror
when it sees itself.
What gets you out of bed,
dancing like a wild purple iris
in the breeze of your next inhalation.
It doesn't matter at all
what you do for a living today.
The priceless jewel is just living.
It doesn't matter at all
how much money you make today.
Your body is more precious than sunlight.
Your sternum is beaten from finer gold.
Whether you feed the multitudes today
or only wash the dishes
makes no difference at all.
What matters is to plunge
down the stem of this unfolding
flower of grace into green meditation,
to follow the thunderbolt in your backbone
all the way home to silence,
and drop the terrible fairy tale
of last week's anger.
Let the mirage of sorrow vanish
in the sky of your chest, empty and blue.
Don't you know that you save the planet
just by being awake?
Love doesn't need a story.

YOU MUST DANCE NAKED

You wear your quietness as a black gown,
woven infinitesimal, every thread
a letter of your silken lover's name.
Your stillness is a trembling
at the touch of invisible lips.
The motion of that kiss has no
first cause, but a stirring
in the groin of loss.

If you want to entice the dawn,
you must dance at midnight.
It is not enough to be empty,
because there is honey
in each cell of darkness
and the tomb is full of wine.

And if your prayer does not imbibe
the moon, the stars, the pit
in the swirl of yearning
with a fiery tongue that tastes
the subtle, ruthless, delicate blade
of love between heartbeats,
then you are not singing
from the center
of your desolation.

Just being quiet and empty
is not enough.
You're still waiting for some God
to say, "Let there be light."

Now burn off all your veils.
Whirl naked in the moment
before you were born.

TIRED OF GODS

I'm tired of gods
who come down from above
and blind us with their fire.
I'm waiting for a god born
from the belly of an earthworm,
with, instead of wings,
fungi cilia flying
underground through hummus,
alchemizing the detritus
of moldering bodies
to live again
and rise into green nipples
for the suckle of hummingbirds
and butterflies.
That too would be a Christ,
a Son, loam-born
of a single Mother.
And the Father?
He would stand Wordless,
bewildered,
barefoot in the mud,
leaning on his ancestral hoe.

SACRED LAND

In our sacred land
there is one most holy day each year,
holier than Christmas or Passover,
holier than Diwali or the end of the Fast,
holier than the Fourth of July
or the Feast of Mick Jagger.

It's the day when every rule is broken,
the past is drowned in forgiveness,
the difference between festival
and meditation gets washed away
by laughter and tears.

It's the day when we gaze namelessly
into the eyes of rival tribesmen
and fall in love with thieves on crosses.
Every prison cell is opened this day.
On this day we smear our faces with chocolate
and drink red wine. On this day we close
our ancient books and dance with valor
among the ruins.

Clothing is optional. Everything is optional.
There is only one law: "Love and do what you like."
The word "no" cannot be spoken.
But this too sounds like a rule, so some folks
just sing "no" all night in holy defiance.

Other days of the year
get soaked in the cream of this day.
God walks on earth this day, because God
is a Man without fear, and a Woman free.

Now I'm sure you are asking, "When
will this day come?" So I'll answer you, friend.
This day is today. Are you ready?
Are you sure?

NON CREDO

I do not believe in my heartbeat.
Yet it thrums on.
I do not believe in my hand
stirring honey into tea, then
washing my grandmother's cup.

In the dance of my fingers
I do not need to believe.
I simply observe and honor them.
Nor do I believe in the taste
of an heirloom pear
from a tree my father planted,
it is so sweet.
Gristling my fist around his original hoe,
I bend to the carrot patch.
I learned this bending from a gracious
willow without believing in trees.

I do not believe in the hummingbird
asleep on a lilac twig, head cradled
on her own emerald breast.
Or in the silken cat slipping
through her element of moonbeams.
I do not believe in your eyes,
yet their gaze obliterates my confusion.
It is enough to hear the stars
falling through my body like snow,
the sound of marrow soaked with breathing.

I do not have a belief, I have a practice.
Bowing to no savior, I just bow.
The word dissolves into silence.
Silence dissolves into action.
Action dissolves into wonder.
At dawn, the mist in a sunbeam.
At evening, the mountain in a cloud.

ODE TO YOUR HANDS

I honor your hands, those skillful
bones, tendons, knuckles, knobs:
you awe me, tool-holder!
I bow to you, my own hands inept,
little accomplishing, hardly able
even to fondle themselves in prayer.
You who tie knots and make shelters,
you who reach into birth blood and turn
the breached foal's head in the womb
of the mare, woodcarver, carpenter,
thrower of pots, blacksmith, diamond
cutter, pruner of fruit trees;
you who swing bats or sink birdies,
loaf kneader, roller of noodles, whirler
of pizza dough; calligrapher allowing
clouds to stain the silken sumi-e,
expressing mountain and bamboo
in wrists and fingertips, I honor you!
Squirting milk into a bucket
from the goat's teat, or fingering
the Uileann pipes as you gaze into
the eyes of Danu, inward Mother
of green Eire; and you, the lonely
cosmetician with your palette of faces
I do not forget, nor you, foot masseuse,
nor plumber, chiropractor, nurse
practitioner laying hands on the sick
at midnight, unknown to the doctor,
or bandaging the leaky toilet pipes,
equally skillful; you the medic, binder
of wounds on the battlefield;
and the veterinarian who skillfully
removes a rubber duck from the belly
of a Labrador; nor do I forget
the greasy engineer in the rib cage
of a tramp steamer at sea,
or the star-fluent navigator
in oceanic night, on the bridge
with his sextant and compass.

I honor the breaker of rusted bolts,
and you who changed my mother's
tire on the highway; you who somehow
lay brick walls in a straight line,
or play the steel-stringed guitar with
tough delicate fingers; poodle groomer,
I honor your hands sword-wielder,
marksman, backhoe driver, shaker
of the shaman's rattle at the moon.
I honor the deft diaper changer
and the mixer of cocktails;
the Ayurvedic pulse-reader,
the miner with infernal drill;
distiller of barley malt, brewer,
grafter of grape vines; you who bless
tinctures and ointments, crushing
flowers into homeopathic salve,
all of you equally adept; I honor
the handyman and midwife, builder
of campfires, mudra weaver in
your mountain shrine, and you
love-maker also, most dexterous.
With my hands, that make nothing,
I offer this poem.

MIDSUMMER'S EVE AND MORNING

Eve

In the longest twilight of the year
I compose an ode to silence -
nothing more than breathless sighing
in green caverns of hydrangea
where sparrows rustle and doze,
a glistening path where the young snail
senses moonlight and inscribes
her patient journey over the roses,
and a blue moth settles on the peony's lips
like a first kiss. Just so,
summer comes without words.

Morning

Like an arrow
the axis of love
pierces the center of a star
and pins it to the dark meridian
of your heartbeat.
Now is the shuddering pause
in our turning wheel
of gratitude.
Any creature who can say "I Am"
is filled with her creator.
There is plenty, therefor be quenched
by yearning.
If you don't understand this
go outside at sunrise.
Listen to the warbler who sings
about the golden splendor
dawning in her tiny breast.

PARTNER

To fall in love with
the same sweet partner
all over again
is possible.
Not through discipline
but mysterious sacraments
of the commonplace,
held hands, rainy pavements,
corner tables,
the grace of the first smile
reappearing
in a wrinkled cheek.
The years are a mirage,
though they shimmer with
sweet memories.
Many lifetimes
of simple kindness
bear fruit.
Tears mean something.

WORLD WITHOUT US

Written during the Covid-19 pandemic of 2020

I'm sorry to say how sonorous earth would be
without us, how clear the voice of streams
plucking their harps of stone,
the waterfall-leaping salmon chant,
goat bleats erupting from the torn
pomegranate of the nanny.
How fresh the smell of rain and sweet
the pollen on the bee's feet, hum
of rummaging among wild roses:
but who would make the Poem?
A dolphin perhaps, or an elephant on the shore,
susurrution of black flies fleeing her swished ear?
A stir in the leaf-languid jasmine, rattle
of palm fronds scenting storm, frolic
of pelicans skimming whitecaps for carp?
A verse of the Poem might be
a logos of waves stroking coral, pink
in the grouper's gaze, his mouth articulating
bubbles in the mindfulness of the shark.
Another, the whirring return of vast hunger
to the belly of the hummingbird. Or rustle
in the pelt of an elk before his bugling stuns
the world back into silence.
How patiently the stars would listen
above the basso continuo of microbes
intoning their restless intuitions.
But who would hear the night itself
and give voice to quietness?
Perhaps the owl, that darkling huntress
zeroing down on her mouse…
Oh the Poem will survive us, surely,
other tongues enunciate the descant
of the blood, wingéd and four-leggéd singers,
free to be their savage selves as we
once were, but humbler, quieter, knowing
beyond knowledge when to stop.

CHANDRA NADI

Drink the full moon.
Hold her as a breath,

then set her back
gently in the sky.

Gaze awhile
and you will see

the blaze of your
own tenderness,

the bruise of your caress.
She loved that.

It awakened her.
Now, with your whole body,

you must teach God
how to kiss.

WHAT HAPPENED TO WELLS

And why have they disappeared?
Or perhaps we just don't see them anymore.
A well in the heath and fen of your body,
under a mossy omphalos of stone.

Every walk is toward or from the goddess
of some local birth-well.
Your flesh is a map of chthonic rivers.
Weeping is a well. The belly. The womb.
In your forehead an artesian well where
pilgrims drink on their journey to the heart.

A well the mouth, the navel, the cave that leads
to the soul in the sacred valley of your thighs.
Have you searched, guided by thirst,
stumbled and broken your urn,
then looked down and there it was! -
on a summer morning, in a pathless
glade of absences?

Under your sternum it bubbles,
a bittersweet spring where atavistic shadows
ferment the vintage of awakening.
How many centuries since some ancestor
drew these waters of solace up?

When you listen to what listens,
your ear is a well, spiraling abysmally inward,
effusing the sound of the sea.
Between your thoughts, silence is a well.
Words are only the stony rim of it.

Never cap the aquifer in your crown.
Burst. Cover the earth. Be a mist.
Yet share not all your living waters.
Keep a secret fountain unfathomably murmuring
in the dark, the faintest breath-stream,
your wellspring of divine aloneness.

JASMINE

Dear one, when you
go, please leave
an echo of your song,
the way a fallen
petal leaves the scent
of jasmine,
so that those who
truly listen
to what's hidden
in silence
will close their eyes
to savor this breath
and hear you call
from deep inside,
"Don't follow,
just dissolve."

ODE TO YOUR HEARTBEAT

Heart has no metaphor.
Rhythm is all, a beat that kneads
its tenderness into every creature
with an open wound,
drumming a circle of comfort for the half moon,
a circle to gather the ebbtide of a thousand suns,
a circle that widens and un-times the moment,
awakening your ancestors,
all their troubles and blessings.
A drum circle in the heart to hug the unborn
like sand grains melting back to Now,
this bubble of hot glass blown into a globe
of fragile beauty.

What your heart beats is not blood only,
but the Milky Way, wild honeysuckle sap,
the DNA of buffalo stirred
into the batter within a cocoon,
from which a herd of winged bulls emerges,
stampeding across the rainbow.
What the heart drums is your pain,
folded into the dough of your body,
when risen, punched down to rise again
into the warm loaf at the oven's core.

What your heart beats is the ocean of motherhood
saturating the placenta, regarded as waste
by the man but food by the earth.
It beats the plasma in a plastic catheter
hanging over the precious struggle
of parted lips that yearn for one last breath.
Heart-beaten also the arterial nectar of Gaia,
thick, black, crude.

Do not disdain the mastodon
whose bones were crushed
into a single drop of death for you.
Do not pretend your heart won't hurt,
or flutter, or lie moist and fibrilant
in the ashes of your cremated flesh.

Yes, sometimes your heart feels like
a hermit organ living in a cave,
pouring the luster of her solitude
into a thousand trillion cells, those tiny mirrors
of distant nebulae, rhymed by your pulse.

Do not imagine that your heart is in
a higher realm. There is no higher.
This is the realm where all worlds kiss,
and finally all beams bend into a sphere.

Nor imagine that your heart can fly.
For the sun has melted these wings
so that you might fall, again and again,
into this vale of salted bones,
where Way itself is lost,
and the heart is the only tavern.
All wanderers rest here, you also
repose, and drink, and listen to their stories,
and hear the silence between the stories,
as you gaze into the fire.

SALMONBERRIES

Here is the good news
for the first Sunday in June.
There is no solution
because your life is not a problem.

Here is the Gospel for a morning
when salmonberries dangle
in their sable caps, lusciously
yellow, surfeit of their own
bright leaves.

If you do not take a handful
and smear them on your tongue
right now, the deer will do it!
They will come so silently to steal
the beauty you cannot see.

Or by a viridescent shadow pool
between the ferns unfolding
in close breathless air,
a huckleberry's sour fire
will succor you.

Taste all that brims and
burns with color.
Given the wild
possibility of such a world,
is this not the best news?

No conclusion, no certain end
or new beginning.
Only pulsation, survival,
and the edgeless unceasing
chaos of faith.

IF YOU PRAY

If you pray because
you believe it will change
the planet, don't waste
one precious breath.

If you pray because
your mind is at war
with the way things are,
then solve your mind,
not the world.

But if you pray because
a bruised defiant bud
breaks open inside you,
these razor-sweet petals,
this mad fragrance
unquenchable, then pray
for me, friend, too.

I exist because you pray.
In all this green and lovely
wounded earth, here am I,
and you have entered
my aloneness.
I need you from afar.

COLLAPSE

It's time for the sacred collapse,
time to dissolve the Big into the Small,
time to pulverize the general into luminous particulars.
Melt guns. Topple steeples. Time to deck
abandoned halls of Congress with honeysuckle,
bee hives, and elk scat, time for herons
and cormorants to roost in shattered window-nooks
over Wall Street, Trump Tower sagging limp
under tangled clumps of morning glory.
Time to replace the Left and Right with multitudes
of whirling olive bodies, let dandelions explode
through the marble floors of Hollywood, the Hamptons,
were once the party of the poor gave dinners
for $50,000 per plate. Time to replace
the federal state and the corporate monopoly
with indominable family farm collectives,
and government bureaucrats with muddy-toed poets.
Time to dismantle the mega-church with all
multi-national banks into a chaos of village dances,
backyard healing circles, cacophony of tortoise rattles,
bone-flutes in the local shaman's nose...
Yes, it's time for the sacred collapse, and the silent
glow of ancient dust the moment after.
Time for the random veneration of pebbles,
indecipherable runes on dragonfly wings, tools you carve
with older tools, using your grandmother's songs.
Time to protect your identity, and back up the data
for 700 past lives in a purgatorial iCloud, then erase it all
with a single breath. Take off your underwear
and smudge with the warm ash of archaic dollar bills.
Use only roots, herbs, tinctures of lavender and yarrow
for currency. I'll let you have my Goldman Sachs
portfolio for six fresh pomegranates.
I'll give you wordless secrets of deep meditation
in exchange for your fireside gaze.

PLEDGE

I pledge allegiance to no flag.
I pledge allegiance to no nation,
no tribe, no party.
I pledge allegiance to no bombs
bursting in air,
but to the silence in a day of prayer.
True patriotism is rebellion.
True rebellion is joy.
Cast down the mighty, the masters of war.
I pledge allegiance to the poor.
I pledge allegiance to hemp and sod.
I pledge allegiance to the unnamed god.
I pledge allegiance to the moon and tide,
to sun and wind and what I cannot know.
I pledge allegiance to the rainbow,
to the light that contains all colors.
I pledge allegiance to living coral.
I pledge allegiance to an heirloom tomato seed
and to the wisdom in the weed.
I pledge allegiance to the unborn
curled in the mother's sea of trust.
I pledge allegiance to the dust.
I pledge allegiance to all winged
and swimming children of the earth,
to creatures that crawl or come out at night,
to all my relations who wait to take birth,
to brothers and sisters, four-legged and two.
I pledge allegiance to you.

GOSPEL

September now.
I hear petals weeping,
singed with their own fire.
I hear seeds grieving lost goldenrod
and mountains gliding home on clouds.
I still follow the glistening pilgrimage
of that old summer snail across the hosta leaf.

Yet I renounced world sorrow
for the hidden pain of love,
gave up charity and pity to gaze
into your face, where I find all
the otherness I can endure.
With a single inhalation,
I bind and heal the wounds
of rich and poor, oppressor and victim.
My brain is busy with forgiveness.

Both chambers of my heart are murmuring
with gratitude: the empty one says thank you
to the one that pours, then offers back
the ancient gift of my grandmother's blood.

My temple is the pillaged garden, my alter the sky.
We hold satsang in the wetlands,
the frogs, blackbirds, and I.
When in doubt I walk barefoot in wet grass
at midnight, un-naming the stars.

Friend, it's not the world that makes you suffer,
but your judgments about it.
And surely, the last judgment
is the silence of a white chrysanthemum
bursting under the Autumn moon.
This is the Gospel of Astonishment.

DO ANY KINDNESS

Do any kindness.
Become a leaf, kiss the asphalt.
If someone with even an ember in their gaze
opens the palm of true wanting,
show them how their hollow hand
already holds the night,
with all its weightless stars.
Remember how to ache and yearn.
Be a stone in the meadow
glistening with crystal fissures
under the moon, a nurse-log
wounded with seedlings,
a chrysalis on the ash twig,
throbbing with distant Spring.
Now plunge into the shadow of grace
cast by the incandescent diamond
of your solitude.
Hear the pulse of your own blood
chanting Thou, Thou, Thou.
Feel every atom as a tumult of patience
awaiting the breath of the feral I Am,
who comes to brush her silken fur
against the glow of second flesh
inside your flesh... And what if
your heart should stop beating?
She would be the midnight where
the snuffed-out flame goes, still infused
with the fragrance of your loss.
She would be nearer than aloneness,
the place inside where prayers begin.
All I have ever wanted to share with you
is this sensation, friend, this kiss
pressed on the mouth of the Beloved
deep in your emptiness,
the tremor of un-knowing
that is your soul.

TRASH: A SABBATH MEDITATION

"All things share one breath, the beast, the tree, the man." ~Chief Sealth

In meditation this morning,
I breathe in stones on which I can find
no names, only numbers marking the graves
of anonymous mental patients who died
in the influenza epidemic at Western State Hospital, 1916.
I breathe in a broken typewriter from my neighbor's trash,
and a tangle of audio tape that was once a Dharma talk
by a now disgraced guru.
I do not believe in progress.
I return to my breath.

In meditation this morning,
I breathe in the sorrows of Christmas,
three used hypodermic needles, two discarded
double-A batteries and an empty zip-lock bag
containing the scent of snow.
I breathe the spilled shell casings from a clip
of hollow-point bullets purchased
on the black market to assassinate policemen.

I breathe the acrid transparency of Commencement Bay,
where according to John Muir, spawning salmon
once crowded fat and thick enough to walk across,
while ten thousand elk bugled on cedar-mazed cliffs,
all subsequently leveled by the Army Corps of Engineers.
I do not believe in progress.
I return to my breath.

70 million years ago I took this breath,
but I have not yet returned it.
Still it gathers praise, laden with thistles
and seeds of henbane, African dream root,

fragrance of blue Egyptian water lily,
lehua spores in lava dust from the sacred island.
An arc of breath bearing two of every kind,
the outflowing and inflowing, the vicious and pitiable,
filaments of scarab wing, ancestors' prayers,
tears of the unborn teeming in deep space,
embryonic constellations soaring
through the zodiac of the egg.

In meditation this morning,
I inhale the whirling souls of the lost,
who cannot find the earth again
for it is beyond recognition.
I inhale microbes laden with DNA
from extinct species, the progeny of the unforgiven.
And I do not forget to breathe your tears
of ruined hope for a better country.

Morning Tonglen practice: all these
ten thousand things I breathe in,
but what shall I breathe out?
Ah, that is not yet known.
I hold this breath in honor of your grieving.
I can only tell you, it won't be stone or plastic,
OxyContin or petroleum dripping from pelican wings.
It must be something luminous, something new,
whispering oceans of ancient moonlight
heaped in the coals of my body.
Something like a Goddess, yet not in heavenly form,
but in the footprint shape of dust
on pilgrim paths that tangle back
to tribal council fires, circle songs of friendship.
And what I breathe out will not be
my breath only, but yours.

WHAT HAFEZ WANTS

Even though we're alone
and grieving a fathomless loss
that we cannot quite remember,
Hafez wants each of us to keep
our tavern open all night.
God is parched.

Hafez wants to teach our wolves to howl,
to teach frolicking and screeching
to our alley cat souls, wants us to drink down
the hollow in the cup.

Here in this ambiguous world, we stumble
on a body at the tip of every shadow.
But we get to choose, at the last moment,
whether to die of rapture or misfortune.

Hafez wants to distil in your eye a single tear
containing the nectar of mourning and ecstasy.
Don't you love this land of bee-mused
vine-tangled labyrinths, each night a different
flavor of the moon, each day's purifying fire
exiled to other hills and valleys of lilac and umber?

You were already drunk when you arrived.
You can't be choosy about who walks you home.
Just for tonight, I've saved seven bottles
of precious love-wine, aged in my chest.

You must help me with them, friend.
We'll work together.
You're parched, I'm parched.
God is parched.
But it's all the same thirst.

A DARK WORLD

When you asked,
How can I face
such a dark world?
the answer was all around you.
Wands of pine
in a soft breeze answered,
bell-throated blackbirds
ringing over the wetland
answered, stars
floating on a still pond
answered, dancing
milkweed like snow answered,
pearl-eyed mushrooms
seeing through the midnight forest
answered: This world
is not the seat of sorrow.
This world is sunlight
playing in the mist
that rises over a fountain
of beauty.
The seat of sorrow is your heart,
aching and thirsting
for its own light.
Yet the healing is easy.
Turn your gaze around
and see into your source.
You are that fountain
of beauty, you are that
mist of the wings of light.
Just listen to a raindrop fall,
how it finds its way
home, as fallen things do,
to a hidden wellspring
under the green and piquant moss
where it was born.
Even the raindrop answers,
Yes.

FUCK UP

Make a delicious mistake. Fuck up once in a while.
After all, I invented peanut butter and jelly sandwiches
when I was 4 years old, stealing and smashing
two jars from mommy's grocery bag, sticking my hands
in the mess, then in my mouth, wiping the glisten
of chunky brown and crimson from my cheeks
with soft white Wonder Bread. Yes I did.

When I was 7 I invented the frisbee
while throwing a plateful of broccoli
my babysitter forced me to eat out the window.
I did. And I invented S'mores at the age of 12
when a pimply camp counselor wouldn't let me
have three desserts: so I crushed them into one.
Don't you love people who crush things into one?
And burn the marshmallow?

Even when I was in utero my great aunt Molly,
who lived in a previous century, made me wear
red rubber rain boots, scrawling on them L and R,
as if knowing left from right would matter to
an epic 8-shaped womb-swimmer who could
circumscribe the galaxy without a single breath!
She made me so angry that my subatomic bones
rattled the stars. Yes, I was a mad and feral embryo.

What did you invent by smearing, by smashing,
by a glorious lack of impulse control
in the sacred mayhem of your childhood?
Go ahead, tell me everything. Or tell
an exquisite lie so outrageous it might be true:

"I invented the way light shatters in the prism of a dewdrop
by powers of ten to create the first rainbow." Or,
"I was a wanderer, hitchhiking before I could walk."

Or this one: "Past sins cancelled all my works of mercy,
negative and positive colliding in my heart and
adding up to nothing, no karma at all, which is why,
at birth, my fetus crowned through Mother's perfect Zero."

Makes sense to me, Friend. Now listen:
Whoever God is, She embraces this mess.
Squirting our mouths with milky streams of life,
and more life, She overbrims our grail with
Second Chances, permitting the Impeccable Blunder.

From the uncertain locus of an electron
to unforgiveable mutations in a molecule of cytosine,
right up the crazy chain of non-causation
to the way black chaos engenders stars
in the belly of a supernova, all of us
are mistakes of necessity, even Jesus, hairline
fractures in the magnanimous vacuum, filled in
with molten gold, kintsugi of the human face.

So if you never got sentenced to time-out chair
in kindergarten, or sent to the principal's office
for pulling someone's pony tail in grade school;
if you never cut class to explore the wilderness
in your soul, or skipped church to attend
the carnival in your flesh; if you never got
tear-gassed by cops on the street in college;

never got fired, never spent a single night in jail;
and never found your body in a hot mess
on the kitchen floor, your fingernails engraving
hieroglyphs of grief in the linoleum: dear one,
you may not actually have lived at all.

MEN

Men who believe women.
Men who care for women in pain.
Men who praise women when
their bodies grow old.
Men who listen to women even when
they repeat themselves.
Men who hear women even when
they do not speak.
Men who grasp whole women
with their hearts,
not parts of women with their hands.
Men who hug women well,
radiance to radiance.
Men who linger by forest ponds
and gaze into green stillness,
speaking to the great Mother.
Men who travel deep into the wilderness
not to hunt or kill,
not to climb the highest peak,
but just to be there.
Men who know valleys,
observing the etiquette of mist,
the customs of cedar and willow.
Men who understand
that the fire in their belly
is the Goddess.

EULOGY FOR A FINCH

I am glad my wife and I
were home that afternoon
when the strawberry-headed finch
flew against our windowpane,
then lay amazed among
the pine cones,
the vast translucent sky
a tiny topaz
in her widening pupil.
We watched her breast,
the color of a withered leaf,
pulse slow, and slow the more,
her black beak groping
for a breeze barely remembered...
Then she was still,
but not alone.
Our presence enfolded her,
tender as the Autumn air
she could not breathe.

MERELY METAPHYSICAL

Emptiness is merely metaphysical.
But loss is a commitment to follow your pain
deep into the heart, until it leaves
your body through the exit-wound.
Become what pierced you,
the arrow floating back to the bow,
the green worm entering
the pit of your sweetness.
Understand that the dark
is not the absence of light.
The dark is the womb of light.
Poised in perpetual equinox,
denser than Osmium, weightless
as the moon, don't be so sure
that you ever got out of the egg.
If you miss the full round foolishness
of Zero, subtract the One.
Be a chrysalis after the larva
dissolves into unknowing.
Perhaps a shimmering rainbow
will unfurl, perhaps not.
Trust uncertainty, the blade between
breathing out and in.
Bend toward Winter now, the mothering
etherium, umbilicus running backward
into the marrow between stars,
which is the silence between your thoughts.
Fall into a rhythm of stillness prior
to the moist immaculate conception
of moss, mycelia, hemlock root,
before your soul can even murmur, "Behold,
I am the handmaid of the Lord."
Your sigh is the desert God crosses at night,
your abandoned prayer the ruined castle
He almost sees in a lazuli mist beyond desire.
Ferment your tears and you may hear
the gentlest sparrow, the cedar whisperer,
a tree frog in thistle-laden wind, all singing
about your fearlessness.

OCTOBER WALK (A PROSE POEM)

The portal to the miraculous is this toadstool. Frog croak, wand of fading lavender, musk of deflated tomato in the devastated garden. These are your talismans, carry them. Honed by loss, don't veer from the edge of your blade. The grit of your destination is the gravel in your path. Fear resists, resistance thickens. Allow your veils to thin.

If you're elder enough, read the purple hieroglyphs in the back of your hand. Love glows from husks. Get hollow. Be starlight through a brittle leaf. Illumine whatever you deeply observe: a quivering nipple of blue chanterelle, ferns remembering to bow, vulva of a broken apple bubbling in a sunbeam, inscrutable runes of the worm among the fallen, some rotting, some ripe.

Poised on the peak of the least sensation, leap into the void from a dendrite's tip, weightless in the grace of dying. Avoid abstraction, just be the witness of fire in a synapse. Whatever arises before you now is the Mandala of Supreme Awakening.

Dip your eyeball in the dew-flame of a pyracantha berry. Through a moonlit spider's web, enter the temple of intergalactic diamond emptiness. Genuflect in moss, letting one silent tear encircle ten thousand cedars. It is important to find this tear and weep.

Your backbone is a scimitar. Buff it with breathing. Let its curve approach the asymptote of otherness. When your exhalation becomes the sky, you will hear a heron shriek over withered cattails, and your heart will erupt with the laughter that created the world.

Not with mind but unshod toes, in the moment of mud where it all began, sense the tremor of genesis. Bathe your mother and father, all your relations, seven generations past and seven to come, in waves of amazement. Stand for nothing but the stinging grass, the wetness.

ESOTERIC MATHEMATICS OF SRI YANTRA

Silence x Grace - Time = Love.
I derived this equation by applying the science of tears
to the field of yearning.
I raised God's name by the power of the Mother
and ascended into a shining exponential cloud
where rocks, bones, roses and prime numbers
have no existence in pure space,
for all appear as multiples of one.
I factored my thought-waves into an empty denominator,
by which I divided a tufted titmouse, a fern,
a dog turd, and a jade Buddha,
which resulted, marvelously enough, in a quotient
of titmouse, fern, dog turd and Buddha,
all things remaining just as they are.
Then I stepped naked into zero-entropy snow
melting in a stream of super-radiant virtual electrons
that spilled from a glacier on Mount Meru,
where I drowned in the gurgling calculus of chaos
between the curve of my inhalation
and the asymptote of silence.
There I beheld the square root of the void
and became the algorithm uniting God and Man,
not through mantric repetitions of the name of Kali,
but a hyper-geometric progression of breaths, wings
and inconceivable sexual epiphanies
in the company of angels,
holographing the One into the Many,
empowered by a logarithm of Negative Zero.
Friend, I think you would do better to solve this equation
by resting your brain on the astrolabe of your heart.
There the rune for love is engraved before conception.
All this information and more than I could ever record
was channeled to me by Albert Einstein,
who still wanders from star to star,
pulling his books and groceries behind him
in a little red wagon.

Note: In tantric yoga, Sri Yantra is a visual portal to meditation consisting of nine interlocking triangles, said to embody the energy of the Goddess creating the cosmos. Old friends in Princeton NJ do recall Einstein pulling his belongings in a Radio Flyer.

GRAND ALIGNMENT

I understand there's quite
an alignment coming.
But if you don't align
your breath and bones,
what use is a horoscope?
Weave this dream
into your handiwork.
The new moon is your forehead,
the daystar your belly,
the total eclipse a trough
between heartbeats.
Your mind is space itself,
shining with the color of silence.
The portal to the coming age
is your body.
Why wait for the conjunction
of Venus and Mars?
These lovers have been
waiting for you
in the bridal chamber
of your chest.
Now ascend to higher worlds
by hugging all your atoms
with this inhalation
while practicing the asana
of a smile.
To be joyful for no reason
is to master all
the planets and stars.

MISSION

You have a deep green mission on a thirsty planet.
To taste the nectar of this breath.
To ransack the meadow with your nose,
scenting honeysuckle in the dark.
To be awake and listening at 4 a.m.,
invoking the quiddity of a thrush.
To see the vanishing beauty of innumerable suns
in a snowflake on your fingertip,
the galaxy we're lost in on a turtle's back,
the Pin-Wheel Nebula, silver-blue in a moth's wing,
a horoscope of frost on your window, revealing
no other moment but now.
This is what angels fell here to feel.
They wonder if it hurts for leaves
to skitter down a sidewalk,
and how, when you rest in your own peculiar rhythm,
your work is stillness.
You've been a marmot lacerated by a trap,
curled in a burrow of scarlet snow,
warmed by the seep of you own essence.
And that is how you learned to heal yourself.
You've been a chafe of sand-grains in a shell,
grown lovely through silence,
condensed to black pearl.
And that is how you learned to ferment your pain.
There was blood on the sheaf, and then on the floor.
But you did not turn your trauma to stone.
You learned that healing comes
from the energy of the wound itself,
not from the story you tell about it.
Don't waste time being anyone but a Lover.
Permeate the loneliness of voiceless creatures
who have all been you before.

Give hope to pilgrims that this moment
is the journey's end.
Teach wanderers to see their shadows
as rays of gold.
Help old men and orphans to prosper
in the empire of impermanence.
Be the gash made whole by staying open.
Do beauty with your hands, but always remember,
peace is not made, it is breathed.
Now you must fall into the cavern
of your ancient brain, descend to the wine cellar.
Taste the blood that Jesus ages into brandy,
oaked in the cask of your amygdala.
You've been braiding your dreams
into a rope for safety. Let it go.
Plummet toward awakening.
Spend an hour of alchemy
in the musty pump-house, kneeling
by the ancient well, where through
crepuscular days and luminous midnights,
newts and bullfrogs bask in the wild
reptilian splendor that your body
wants more than a soul.
This is the place called the heart,
the portal of the ordinary.
There is no other way
to get through this miracle.
Part the almond-scented serpent skin.
Enter gently, muttering this spell,
"Amen, amen, all things dissolve
into themselves."
Is your mission clear?
Who you strive to become
is not nearly so lovely as who you are.
These are simple words, my friend,
but they were born of many tears.

A SIMPLE RELIGION

My religion is simple.
Let us pray.
The Second Coming is a scavenger kitten
trembling in a flashlight beam
at my pantry door.
My Patron Saint is the half-blind abuelo
carefully cramming his cages of hens
into the luggage rack on the midnight flight
from Newark to San Juan.
My revelation the wail of a newborn citizen
whose mother crossed over
the border last night, her final sigh
a one-word prayer:
"Al Norte."
A free-fallen creature, I drown each day
 in the sea of Grace.
From what must I be saved?
The taste of a broken heart is my bread,
the darkness between ideas
my communion wine,
in the rising and falling of my chest,
the whole story of my Salvation.
The sound of a midnight owl could be
the end of time, a dogwood bud
the Parousía.
Every morning I make a pilgrimage
into my backyard.
The mountaintop is wherever I am.
Look! Barefoot prophecies of dew
in a wilderness of fungi.
I bow to receive a blessing from the ladybug,
priestess of the clover cathedral.
Nose deep between mushrooms, I gaze
into the glittering empyrean of hummus and peat.
I share the grand epiphany
with an eremitic earthworm.
My religion is simple.
Let us dig.

SHRAPNEL

I was wounded in this battle too.
There are bits and pieces
of the world in my vital organs.

Yes, such pain, but the doctors say
it might endanger the heart
to remove them.

So we carry on as best we can,
with fragments of ourselves
lodged in each other's bodies.

FALLING INTO MY SKIN

I am grateful for my skin. It may be edgeless,
and the farthest fractal of my holo-bodhi-gram
is merely blinding diamond consciousness
with neither form nor color, still,
I am grateful for my flesh, roseate, brown
or wheaten, peach, mahogany,
with crow's feet and frown lines, and yet,
I am not God, but what God is.

Grateful for my lymph nodes, sinews, fat,
for bonefulls of dark energy, their marrowed
burrows where the mighty worms and larvae
shall feast one day; and grateful that my plasma
will coagulate into the flan of magots.

Grateful for the live volcano of my basal ganglia,
reptilian gangsters dwelling in my hippocampus,
neuroplastic salamanders of my intuition,
flicking out their twin sulfuric tongues,
for axons and dendrites copulating in caves of fire.

I am especially grateful for my crevices and pits:
Romanesque intestinal corridors, the pagan granaries
of my belly, my windpipe snoring Buxtehude,
the chthonic spiraling mollusk of my inner ear
which contains the ocean of listening,
and the infinitesimal sky within a synapse,
enceinte with embryonic constellations -
the Dolphin, Unicorn, Moth, and Griffon,
stillborn, starless, whose points shall be connected
by flung threads of silken hope, and I will surely
see them when I learn to gaze beyond the void.

For the aurora borealis in my bowels
I give thanks, and I am grateful for the kindly
sun who lights the firmament between my teats,

the Christ jewel in each inhalation, rising
over the horizon of my diaphragm,
sparkling through the rain forest of my alveoli.
And I am grateful for the domed cathedral
of my eyeball, rose window latticed with veins
of second sight, where fugitive tomorrows
find sanctuary, bearing witness of a world to come.

I am grateful for my thin etheric yarmulke,
infant unhealed tenderness of my skull,
where beams of Me still float into the firmament,
a milky braid that pours up into night.
There I still ascend, and from there, fall.
That rope I climb, hand over mind
to the moon, to the sun, to the chocolate
whirlpool of Andromeda, the cauldron
of sweetness, kaleidoscopic doorway
to the waltz of nebulae, unnumbered
sparks of Me, a swarm of possibilities,
trace particles of my soul, who am not God,
but what God is, forever spinning
until I fall, and falling, remember
the atom, the gristle, the bone...

Now in the Winter woods, the deer
are not waiting for Christmas.
They are Christmas. And you?
Are you waiting for the birth of astonishment?
From far beyond the ever-expanding
starry rim of a sphere you cannot conceive,
the light of the grace you shall become
is already falling on your body.

FOOL

Fools take refuge in this moment.
One lightning bolt of wonder
through the belly of a child
incinerates ten thousand books
of philosophy.
The speeches of politicians burn
to tasteless ash in the diamond eye
of a lover.
There is no war in this meadow.
A wild hyacinth springs
from the manure pile, fragrant
with the exhalation of worms.
Angels no longer care if we
believe in them or not.
They yearn to be born on earth
for one cool April morning
just to watch a poppy burst.
But it's never enough, is it?
Soon you want to be reborn
in Winter, just to take
your mittens off and feel
snowflakes melting in the blush
of raw warm palms.
This soul is the infinite distillation
of the senses.
Haven't we been fools
not to taste God, touch God, smell
God's scent, discern God's music
in the silence of the heart?
There is no war in this meadow.
Haven't we been fools
not to breathe God's breath
through every atom of our brief
bewildered impeccable body?

LIES

As soon as I speak your name, I lie.
And if I call you the nameless, I lie.
When I say "Thou" it is a lie,
but saying "I" is a bigger lie.
If I say "Two" it is almost the greatest lie,
but "One" is the mother of lies.
My lies reveal the beauty you cannot
gaze upon, because it is You.
My lies reveal the small blue scentless
violet of your face, blossoming
through a razor-thin fissure
in the sidewalk.
My lies reveal the warm brown hills
of your rump and shoulders,
the dark fast-moving stream that looks
so still in your canyon, the flash
of exhilaration on your warrior's sword,
the scent of your milk on an infant's lips.
My lies burn the shame out of your skin.
They teach you to see this world
through the enso of an unfallen tear.
Saying "thank you" is also a lie.
A mighty gratitude encircled the stars
before you were born.
But my greatest lie is the eye of God
gazing back at you from the mirror
of your own divine silence.
Shiva! Shiva! Shiva! This dance of lies!
This poem of lies!

THE HEALING

This planet will not
be healed
by powerful politicians
in big cities
who spend trillions on
a global strategy
that never quite begins.
They also burn much fuel.
Earth will be healed
by villagers who sing,
by backyard gardeners
like you
who walk more slowly
right here,
who feel the green
through bare soles,
speaking fewer words,
cradling
each others anger
like mothers,
awakening
the heirloom seeds
of the heart.

IMPORTANT TO SAY

It is important to say
that the sun does not caress
this mossy stone without delight,
and the breeze does not ripple
a pond in the meadow without rapture.
All night in the fern forest, a fairy
ring of mushrooms gazes at the moon,
eyes more ancient than ours,
and not without their acid tears of dew.
Important to say how the fallen
forget their trees, to bruise and surrender
their soul of gold to eonian sod,
and not without that peculiar sorrow
which is the heart of time.
Before I leave this place, it is important to say
that I have heard the voice of the raven,
wise as the silence that was here
before God shouted, "Light!"
And I have seen the whole blue curve
of the cosmos in a robin's egg.
I want you to marvel at the grace of the small,
the yearning in the sepal of the last dahlia,
the pebble's presence.
I want you to hear each creature crying,
"I am patience in a stone, ardor in a seed,
the whisper of grief in a meadow of scattered bones.
We are from the stars and they are not cold.
Loam is alive with all our relations,
Mitákwe Oyasin!
And the vast empty night, even when you think
you are alone, is awake, awake
and not without love, a vigil unto itself,
like you, silently tenderly burning."

TO REMIND YOU

To remind you of the soft
explosion in your chest,
the Goddess of the hollow
invented flowers.
Gaze into wisteria, return
to the lapis bayou where the elders
dance on their roots and unborn
children swim toward you.
Did she not create your face
to temper the blinding night of her counsel
as you receive them?
What you call falling, she calls the waltz.
What you call a wrong note,
she calls stunning harmony.
You say mistake, she says creation.
Now take off the veil of doubting.
See in the dark.
Within this absence of noise
is another kind of silence,
the throb of her fingers
on the lute of your spine,
the tremor of a poem
before its first line.
She is the sound in the word "friend"
when it is not spoken.
This is how Mary comes to your sepulcher.
She wants to trouble the sun
that sleeps in your bone dust,
wants to wander in your garden
at dawn, her stillness
whetting the blade of this breath
to cleave your heart in two,
one chamber for her,
the other for you.

OUTLAW

Be an outlaw like Jesus, a swashbuckler
like Krishna, wearing peacock feathers
and prancing on the razor blade
that severs bliss from happiness.
Be the Coyote disguised as a guest
at the wedding, sidling up to the wine bar.
Or a desperado like the Prophet,
but don't rob caravans
unless you can show everyone,
both rich and poor, impeccable respect,
convincing even kings to travel light.
Or become a bandit like the Guru,
who empties your mind and leaves
only a dot between your eyebrows.
Once you encounter the lawless one
you'll live dangerously, heeding
no rule but kindness, no practice but joy.
Other signs of an outlaw?
The swirl of stars above your fontanelle.
The golden temple in your rib cage
with an alabaster door whose key
is wonder, leading to the place
where you were never born.
A Goddess dancing on your belly button.
Feeling more at home when you're lost.
Following every commandment
without even knowing it's there.

BARE BRANCH

Wind moved the bare branch
at my window, scratching
random runes on frosted glass.
I did not attempt to interpret them.
Their meaning simply appeared
in Winter awareness
like black flames on white
scrolls of silence.
This is what the wind said.
Aloneness is the dream,
all-oneness the awakening.
Here is your hardest lesson.
The conflict you perceive
is the conflict in your mind
made visible by grace,
that you may learn through images
and reflections how
your own thoughts bind you
until you let them go.
Be mad and free.
Be naked, sky-like and empty.
Laugh, sing, dance, cry.
You are the cause of Spring.

A MORATORIUM ON NAMES

I have been in love for seven million years.
It was always you. Don't ruin it now
by telling me your name. It is time
for a moratorium on names,
so that we can finally see each other.

A moratorium on the name of God
and the name of Peace, until we learn
to use them both as verbs. A moratorium
on the name of Love, so that this body
may be love's most exquisite synonym.
A moratorium on Better and Worse,
Heaven and Hell, so that our eyes may
grow accustomed to the earth.

A moratorium on the sobriquets of Christ, Krishna,
Allah, Yahweh, giving the goddess breathing room,
that we may hear her inscrutable susurras
from the cavern of the Prophet in each human heart,
infinitesimal thunder in a violet's bell, rung
by a dewdrop. Isn't it time to reinvent the tongue,
babbling sweet new names for the Ineffable?

Intergalactic Hummingbird Silence.
Diamond Gaze of the Holographic Dragonfly.
Tantric Kiss on the Tourmaline Pituitary.
Wastrel's Face in the Bottom of the Empty Grail.
Quantum Spider of the Long-Legged Ayin Soph.
She-Wolf who Suckles My Heart on the Milk of the Forest.
Crocus-Footed Goddess of Melting Snow.
Worm of Delight in the Apple of Melancholy.
Abyss of the Lily in the Light of Dawn.
Magdalenic Desolation.

PIE (MORE CONFUSION ABOUT MY CHAKRAS)

All my chakras vanished
when I tasted the Self.
Now I'm a rose-apple pie,
too caramelized and sticky
to have a subtle body.
Meditate on my flavor, friend,
all sweet and sour and
cinnamon flesh.
I have no recipe.
This crust was cooked with tears.
Let's savor each other and forget
those esoteric Dharma talks,
those secret books of tantra.
Who knows how the heart gets baked
until it is soft and risen,
but I'm sure it's made
with real butter.
Who knows if there is a higher world
than this one with its
Winter wheat and valiant weeds
still blossoming in my ravaged garden.
But I'm perfectly sure
about one thing.
On a honey-golden stamen tip,
the earth is just a pollen speck
in the flower of Now.

VOCATION

When I discovered the emerald
hidden in my ribs
I gave up duty and skill,
wealth, adventure, and fame,
just to follow my menial
vocation: I became
a Jewel Polisher!
I keep moving the ragged cloth
of this breath,
moistened with the tincture
of mindfulness,
over the chalice in my heart
until its golden void
becomes wine, each drop
a gem of insouciance
reflecting a world without edges,
where meadow and forest,
the wreathe of clouds,
the incandescent blackness
of panther night in the eye
of the unhoused stranger,
even the lips of the lover
who lies beside me, are all
one nimbus gleaming
from my cleft lungs.
Now consider that you also
might mother a new creation
just through this work
of being still.

THE AMAZEMENT OF GARDENERS

To the amazement of gardeners, buds open by themselves.
Fallen petals navigate our woodland streams: we call it "drifting."

Ease cures dis-ease, wind-risen grace-lit wings unbeaten.
No warm breath expires that will not lift some other loneliness.

Who shouted "ooze" to the grape, "ferment" to the nectar?
Don't make up stories about it. Ordinary magic simply befalls:

Your gift of ruby-scented madness, the flowering galaxies in your
eyeballs, the inconceivable juice that drips down your spine

when lightning pierces your dreams. Pour out half love's vintage
in libation. Keep the rest in the chalice of your skull.

Drink and stay thirsty. Old Basho and Danté, Laldev and Rabia
tried to tell you this: Entropy conceals a secret counter-force

that orders all things through hidden laws of wonder,
organizing the void into chrysanthemums, the faces of children.

Be quiet now, listen for the voice of your Comforter.
She is the axis of all that spins, deeper inside you than a heart.

The generosity of the dance? She flings planets out of stillness,
with no intent of ever getting them back.

Then, abandoned by your hope, She recedes into the Ineffable,
over the widening rim of the last event-horizon, calling

your name once again, sending like an ark of rescue
that ancient whisper, wave-beaten by the weathers of eternity,

barnacled with all the stars: "No need to try so hard, my child.
Love has already happened!"

RETURN

Through with the big corporation.
Through with the nation-state.
Through with the global church,
the world guru.
Ready to taste the sparkling teats
of the un-miraculous, the near,
I shall be of no creed or party,
neither the Left nor the Right;
the Center, yes, but without
circumference.
Better to barter a bushel of peas
for a well-honed axe handle,
graze my sheep in the commons with yours,
sacred pasture at the village heart.
Our little farms touching in a meadow,
we'll send bees back and forth like letters
in a country with no border but the stars,
a land without minarets or temple spires,
only treetops, Raven Mother perched
in a cottonwood, Father Heron
guarding a nest in the oak,
calling us to lauds and evensong.
Let every forest have its holy writ
in the bio-regional alphabet of leaf veins,
each valley its votive drum-dance
and ancestral bonfire, changing
the bones of our dead into the sky.
I think there shall be eight billion gods,
each with a human body.
Love is local, yet its breath sweeps
moons across the night.
I will dance like a flame in you kiln,
you like a pear on my table.
Every house a temple, every child a priest,
every flower an offering, and every word a prayer.
So in each shall be increased
the mystery that is everywhere.

WOUNDED FLUTE (TO RUMI)

We met on a pilgrimage to stillness,
seated on the same donkey, every atom
of my flesh an oasis, every atom of yours a well.
When we gazed at each other, we could not speak,
because our mouths were filled with one sky.
Still our hearts broke with that sound, the scratch
of brittle leaves against the prison window.

When the breeze blew out of the East, how those
iron bars rang with sweet songs of exile!
If we did not hone our loins with stabbing tears
of ancient friendship, how could poems seep
from our jagged bones, like the wine Jesus served
at dawn, when all the other guests had departed?

Nothing caused this radiance between our ribs;
we simply gave up trying to arrive.
Yet beauty is more lovely half-veiled, seen
by one whose eyes have been polished by waiting.
Thus that night near Konya, when you danced
at the edge of the meadow in rags of moonlight,
among frog songs and blackberries...

Are we not a broken mala, whose scattered beads
became the stars, and our minds the silence
between them, though the thread is still tethered
to the sacrum, where the pain of yearning gushes up?
So this wounded flute makes music, because it has
been torn like yours from a living branch
with seven gashes for the song-maker's breath.

All wounds widen into one ancestral emptiness.
Everyone receives them, yet in different places.
They keep us open to the gift of the Beloved's absence,
the grace of the One, floating on her ocean of zeros.
Which must be why the purest prayer
is simply "O!"

BRUISE

If She does not wound you here, in the soft tissue
between heartbeats, how can you say that you have met
the Teacher? And how will you know when She comes?

Your emptiness turns indigo, your darkest places overflow
with musk. There's a bruise in your crown that never quite heals,
and when you breathe through it, your bones fill up
with orphaned lightning. Infinite things become finite
so that you can pluck them. Stars borrow your sobriquet,
receiving permission to blossom in your father's meadow,
where the sun becomes a firefly for one perfect evening.

Mushroom forests spread their odor through your arteries.
Your nerves wild berry vines, each grape ferments before
the picking. No one tends this vineyard. You fallow wild,
edges unplucked, feckless and delectable, where wanderers
and pilgrims eat their fill. In your chest is a gash.

It's lips move without speech. Scenting the smudge
of your longing, friend and stranger lie down within you,
to fall not quite asleep, but gently pulse in your stillness,
like worlds before creation. No one moves through the valley
of grace without these lacerations, this shattering of light
into shards of darkness gleaming like spilt wine, the wine
of which many speak but few have tasted, neither bitter
nor sweet, but salty, like the gristle of a shadow.

Instead of slumber, a waveless blue flame trembles
all night through your granary of tears, burning
the oil of grief, whose fragrance is love.
How often must one grail break against another
before you remember that this smoldering in the soul
is your body, and you cease to pray for light,
because the midnight stillness under your breastbone
has become a maelstrom of stars; and the dignity
of this inhalation, how it softly places the spirit
in each cell of your flesh, is your Lover's secret name?

SONNET IN AUTUMN AIR

A naked breath and all is silken clear:
the ash leaf crinkled by October sun,
the caterpillar's need to disappear
in rainbow dreams of trembling darkness, spun
by uncreated wings in the cocoon,
the sweet diaphanous allure of thread
between a sleepless spider and the moon
entangled like a specter of the dead.
Now split an Autumn gourd and smell the musk
of emptiness, the dim pain we must feel
and savor deep beneath our ruddy husk.
Taste every shadow sunlight might reveal,
and stay where shriveled berries are reborn.
One pure nectar seeps through rose and thorn.

THANK YOU

Thank you water.
I love you rain.
Thank you loam, I love you.
Molder down.
Thank you sun, dawn or evening,
clothe me in your beams.
Thank you, death, you feed the dust
with bodies large and small.
I return to you.
O stars, I'm not sure what you do,
but without you, would I imagine?
I love you, held or falling.
Thank you, masked workers
in orchards or trucks at 5 a.m.
I love you, bruising your hands
with fruit.
Thank you wind.
I receive you like a moaning pine.
You lift me like a thistle.
In elder foolishness I see
my body as an alder leaf.
Autumn comes, hollowing
a place for the soul in things,
for my soul, parched with praising.
Now and always I would
sing like a wren,
disturbing the great silence.

HOW TO FALL ASLEEP

Rest your head on the pillow.
Rest your mind in the heart.
Breathe out the day.
Breathe in the dark.
Be held.

ACKNOWLEDGMENTS

Gratitude to artist Marney Ward for her cover painting of himalayan poppies entitled "Lingering Light." Her website is www.marneyward.com. Versions of some poems have been published in journals such as *Empty Mirror*, *Tiferet Journal*, *Pangolin Review*, *SAND (Science and Non-Duality)*, *The Braided Way*, and in *The Fire of Darkness*, a coffee-table art book I produced with Hawaiian artist Rashani Réa. 'Ancestry' is included in two anthologies: *Inspiring Forgiveness* from Wisdom Publications, and *Poems of Mindfulness* (in Korean) from Suo Books. 'World Without Us' is included in the anthology, *Oxygen: Parables of Pandemic* from River Paw Press.

NOTES

Some ask whether these poems express the spirituality of the East or the West. They express the confluence of both streams in one eternal wave of divine Breath.

I owe inexpressible gratitude to two masters of meditation and their lineage, the Shankaracharya tradition of India. I have spent intimate time with both of them. The first, Maharishi Mahesh, has passed away. Yet I have continued to practice his simple gift of Transcendental Meditation every morning and evening for 52 years. The second teacher, Sri Sri Ravi Shankar, was originally his disciple. For the last 32 years I have supplemented the pure silence of meditation with his healing breath practice, known as Sudarshan Kriya.

Longing to understand the relationship of their wisdom to my Christian heritage, I followed the Medieval pilgrimage routes through France in the 1970s, and finally met another teacher, Mary Magdalene, at a tiny monastery in Provence, near the cave where she spent her contemplative life after the death of Jesus. There I studied the Christian mystics, fed by the Holy Eucharist, and learned the art of Gregorian chant, which carries the human breath back to God. Through direct experience, in that tiny 9th Century chapel among apricot groves, I realized that the inward energy of awakening, bestowed by the masters of Yoga, is precisely the same power who is the Holy Spirit in Christianity. There is not an Eastern breath or a Western breath, but one breath of God, animating all sentient life. Later, at seminary, I studied the scriptures in Hebrew and Greek, while continuing my exploration of Sanskrit. I respect the discipline of good schooling; but it was not scholarship, it was direct mystical experience, that gave me my real education.

Mystics of the East may speak of Shiva and Shakti, while mystics of the West may speak of Christ and the Spirit, but these names refer to the same grace, the power that unites the soul's yearning for God, to God's yearning for the soul, in the Bridal Chamber of the human heart. And the heart is no metaphysical concept. It is this pulsing organ, this flowing wound of love, in the core of our flesh.

Whether I say, "Jai Guru Dev," or "Thanks be to God," my gratitude is one exhalation, leading me back to the source, whose beauty I want to share with you.

ABOUT THE AUTHOR

ALFRED K. LAMOTTE has authored three volumes of poetry with Saint Julian Press. He has co-authored three books of artwork and poetry with Hawaiian artist and spiritual teacher, Rashani Réa. An interfaith college chaplain, meditation teacher, and instructor in World Religions, with degrees from Yale University and Princeton Theological Seminary, he lives on the shore of the Salish Sea, near Seattle WA, with his wife Anna.

Visit his Amazon author page at: *amazon.com/author/alfredlamotte* and meet him at his blog site, "Uradiance": *http://yourradiance.blogspot.com/*

Type Settings & Fonts:

PERPETUA TILTING MT
GARAMOND – Garamond

www.ingramcontent.com/pod-product-compliance
Lightning Source LLC
Chambersburg PA
CBHW080604170426
43196CB00017B/2898